ON THE ROAD WITH
# Slim

CW01464341

# ON THE ROAD WITH
# Slim

## John Elliott

ABC
BOOKS

Published by ABC Books for the
AUSTRALIAN BROADCASTING CORPORATION
GPO Box 9994 Sydney NSW 2001



*First published August 2002*



National Library of Australia
Cataloguing-in-Publication data
Elliott, John, 1951–

On the road with Slim.

ISBN 0 7333 1050 8.

1. Dusty, Slim, 1927– Performances. 2. Dusty, Slim, 1927– Journeys. 3. Elliott, John, 1951– Journeys. 4. Country musicians – Australia – Biography. 5. Country musicians – Australia – Pictorial works. I. Australian Broadcasting Corporation. II. Title.

781.642092

*Designed by Avril Makula,* GRAVITY AAD
*Set in 10.5pt Birka*
*Colour reprodution by Colorwize Studio Pty Ltd, Hilton, South Australia*
*Printed in Singapore by KHL for Imago Productions (F.E.) Pte. Ltd.*

5 4 3 2 1

**PHOTOGRAPH OPPOSITE TITLE PAGE** is of Barry Thornton's Gibson – the guitar responsible for establishing the distinctive Slim Dusty bush-ballad guitar sound
**PHOTOGRAPH OPPOSITE** is of Slim and Joy with their children Anne and David

Dedicated to Slim and his family – thanks for the music,
the friendship and the good times on the road

# Foreword

John Elliott and I are great mates. We've done a lot together and when we get on the road we just cruise into gear; his camera comes out, so do my guitar and hat, and away we go.

In the ten years we've known each other we've seen a lot of country and met a lot of people. John was there to photograph a brand new baby girl who caused her proud parents to miss my show one night over in Western Australia. Her name is Dusty Rose Davis and, by arriving a bit early, she cancelled out her mum and dad's seats at the concert.

John knows more about me than I do myself, and he is not backward in coming forward when anyone needs some briefing on who I am, what I am and how to get to know me.

So, he has pictured me here ... warts and all! I don't know that I approve of all the tales he has told you but I guess 'the truth will come out'. Good on you, John.

Slim Dusty, April 2002

LEFT Slim and the author at a roadside tank near Charters Towers in north Queensland

# Contents

# Acknowledgments

I gratefully acknowledge all those who have helped me to bring this book into being. First, a big thank you to Slim and Joy for inviting me to travel with them over the years. Thanks to Slim's writers, Tony Brooks, Kelly Dixon, Tom Oliver, Joe Daly and the late Stan Coster for their friendship and insights. Thanks to Tony Harlow, Chris O'Hearn, David Baxter, Leon Concannon and the crew from EMI. Thanks also to Arthur Laing, Bob McMinn, Chris Jensen, Rick Aitchison, Ron Adsett and Keith Jamison for their valuable input. Thanks to John Anderson and Arif Chowdhury of EMI Music Publishing. Thanks to Stuart Neal and Brigitta Doyle of ABC Books for their faith. Thanks to Toula, Terry, Reid, Tahnee, Marina and Herman for their patience.

PHOTOGRAPHS

All contemporary photographs are by John Elliott with the exception of the following: page vi by Joy McKean, page xii by Randy Larcombe, page 3 by John Arnold. Historical photographs are used with the permission of the Slim Dusty Archive.

LYRICS

'Highway Blues', 'Biggest Disappointment', 'Gum Trees by the Roadway', 'Travellin' Guitar', 'The Long Road', 'Born to be a Rolling Stone' and 'Just Going Home' reproduced by kind permission of EMI Music Publishing Australia Pty Limited.

'Another Day Another Town', 'On the Move Again', 'Finally Made It Home', 'What am I Doing in this Town?', 'The Front Row', 'Walk a Country Mile', 'The Biggest Disappointment', 'The Road is Still my Home', 'I've Been There and Back Again', 'Travellin' Still, Always Will' and 'I Need to Find a Place' reproduced by kind permission of Slim Dusty Enterprises Pty Ltd.

'Memory Motel' reproduced by kind permission of Alistair Jones.

We acknowledge Rod Boucher as the writer of Traveller's Prayer.

# Introduction

I was born in Blackall, in central western Queensland, and spent the first fifteen years of my life there. The next town was a hundred kilometres away and there was no television and not much rain. My early years were spent fishing at the Blue Hole on the Barcoo River or catching crawchies in the bore drains near the town. My mates and I were always looking for adventure. We lived on the edge of town so it wasn't too difficult to get to the gidgee scrub just out of town. We would ride our bikes as far as we were game. I remember once Llewellyn Hillier and I rode fifteen kilometres out along the Barcaldine road; that was what we called a big adventure at the time.

The highpoints of my week were meeting the train on Saturdays and Wednesdays and checking out any newcomers to our town. During the winter months, football teams from nearby towns would come to play and this always delivered some excitement. The annual show was also thrilling and larger than life. The real highlight was a visit from a circus or a travelling show of musicians. The circus would always play on the flat behind the Tattersall Hotel and the variety shows would set up in the Memorial Hall.

My favourite show was the Slim Dusty Show. Our family would get dressed up and head down to the hall and wait in eager anticipation as the lights dimmed and the show began. It was magical. We would laugh hysterically at the comedy spots, which featured Mulga Dan, and enjoy the music, especially Slim's songs. I was amazed to hear him sing about where I came from. Songs like 'By a Fire of Gidgee Coals' and 'Catching Yellow Belly in the Old Barcoo'.

In the mid '60s I liked the music that was coming from England, especially the Beatles, but in my heart Slim's music still struck a chord. A few years later I worked at radio station 4LG in Longreach and hosted a Saturday night request show called Ranch

LEFT Slim and the author taking a break at Silverton, near Broken Hill

**FAR RIGHT** Slim
and the author at
the photo shoot for
the cover of Slim's
100th album, taken
on a sandhill just
outside Wentworth
on the Murray River

Club. Every week I would get hundreds of letters from listeners requesting their favourite songs. It was no surprise that most people requested Slim Dusty songs. My life was charmed – I was getting paid to play Slim's music. Little did I realise that years later I would also get to travel with and photograph Slim.

In the early '90s *Who Weekly* commissioned me to photograph a Slim Dusty concert at Carlton Hill Station in the Kimberley. On this trip I produced the cover shot for *Ringer from the Top End* and also took a snapshot of Slim and Edna Everage that years later would be used as the signature image for the opening of the National Portrait Gallery. The time at Carlton Hill was to mark the start of a ten-year relationship with Slim that would have me photograph ten CD covers for him and accompany him to most parts of Australia, the Solomon Islands, and even Nashville, USA. Through these years I have come to know Slim as a mate.

Slim is an amazing man. He is more passionate about his music and his fans now than he has ever been. There is no slowing down for this iconic Aussie. Australia Post

got it right when they named Slim 'a living legend'. Even with Slim's amazing record of 103 albums (and still counting), his unprecedented sales success and the adoration of all Australians, there is still a bit of 'the boy from Nulla Nulla' in Slim.

Slim occupies a very special place in Australian music. While Tex Morton and Buddy Williams were making music a couple of years before Slim, it was Slim who took authentic country sounds to a national audience. Slim really paved the way for all Australian artists who came after him, even those in the rock area – for instance, Dave Gleason, lead singer of the Screaming Jets, admits that Slim inspired him to sing with an Australian accent. Apart from our indigenous music, the Australian bush ballad is the only uniquely Australian genre and we have Slim Dusty to thank for helping define and popularise the genre.

Slim Dusty has built his career on the remarkably close relationship he has with his fans. Every year for more than five decades Slim has taken his music to most of Australia. Slim has told me that he will often look down from the stage and recognise everyone in the front row. He goes back year after year to keep his fans happy. On the road, his first priority is to satisfy his fans.

*On the Road with Slim* will take you on a journey with Slim. It will show you another side of the man who has spent much of his event-filled life on the road. The road is Slim's home and I am thankful to Slim for welcoming me into his home.

Enjoy the journey!
John Elliott

**RIGHT** Slim's
ever-present hat on
his well-travelled
guitar case

# Dusty and the Dame

## 1992

Put Slim Dusty and Dame Edna Everage together in the outback and anything is likely to happen. But bush people don't need much of an excuse for a party, so when Susan Bradley of the Carlton Hill Station in the Kimberley announced that Carlton Hill would celebrate its centenary by paying tribute to Slim Dusty's lifetime of recording, word spread fast.

**LEFT** In the Carlton Hill bull catcher, a modified four-wheel drive that the ringers use to chase and catch bulls

The highlight of the celebrations was to be a concert, organised to take place beside a billabong in Carlton Hill's beautiful gardens. It was a magical setting for such an event – this historic cattle station covers 404 700 hectares, while the homestead itself is on the banks of the mighty Ord River.

More than a thousand people turned up for the party and they came from all over – property owners from the Northern Territory and Western Australia, corporate high-flyers from Perth, locals, tourists and dedicated fans all spread their swags on the lawns and got into the spirit of the night. Things kicked off as the sun set over the Kimberley and the crowd gathered by the side of the billabong.

Slim and his band, along with Joy McKean and Anne Kirkpatrick (Slim's wife and daughter), Troy Cassar-Daly, and Ernie Bridge and his band were all there for this very special occasion. But the icing on the cake was the presence of Aussie legend Dame Edna Everage, who hosted the evening's entertainment.

As is typical of most things in the bush the schedule for the night's entertainment was a pretty casual affair – there are no rigid timetables in the Kimberley. Slim and his friends kept the crowd well entertained, but as the night went on the program was running later and later. The stage, a beautifully decorated trailer section of a semi-trailer, served its purpose well but performers' facilities were rudimentary. The nearest toilets were about a hundred metres away in the Carlton Hill homestead.

Slim and Edna, still running on Sydney time, had prepared themselves for the evening's performance and made their way backstage in plenty of time for their allocated slot on the program. They waited and waited in the nippy spring night air.

The combination of the delay and the coolness of the evening was too much for Dame Edna's bladder. She held on as long as she could but in the end had to give in and, doing what any lady would do in the circumstances, discreetly walked to the corner of the hessian fencing backstage, hitched up her glamorous, glittering frock and answered nature's call.

The thought crossed my mind to reach for my camera and capture the event for posterity but commonsense won out in the end. I could very easily have had a saleable photo but the thought of being hounded by Dame Edna's minder Barry Humphries or, worse still, Les Patterson for the rest of my life was too much.

**RIGHT**  On stage with local bush balladeer Ernie Bridge

**BELOW**  On the banks of the Fitzroy River, chatting to a local about the best place to hook a fish

**RIGHT** Dame Edna
Everage whipping
the ringers into a
frenzy

I did eventually take a simple snapshot of Slim with Dame Edna backstage that night and I knew instantly that I had captured two true Australian icons. The photo shows Dame Edna and Slim, arm in arm, beaming joyfully straight into the camera. It is a great shot of both of them and I think it says a lot about our culture. Where else in the world would you get a drag queen housewife superstar and a legendary bush character displaying such public intimacy?

Years later, when I read that Australia was to have its own National Portrait Gallery, to be housed in the old Parliament House in Canberra, I dug out the shot of Slim and Dame Edna and showed it to Andrew Sayers, director of the gallery. Andrew showed remarkable good taste and purchased the picture, which he eventually

*Where else in the world would you get a drag queen housewife superstar and a legendary bush character displaying such public intimacy?*

used as one of the signature images for the opening of the gallery. Slim and Edna also graced the invite from the Prime Minister to the opening.

Slim and his band were in fine form that night at Carlton Hill Station, playing up a storm from the back of the truck in a beautiful bush setting. Over the years I have seen Slim perform hundreds of times and

**ABOVE** Members of
Slim's Travelling
Country Band
getting up close and
personal with Dame
Edna. From left,
Alistair Jones, Ian
Simpson and Mike
Kerrin

that performance in the Kimberleys would go down as one of Slim's best ever.

That night he seemed to give his all. Slim is competitive by nature and always rises to a challenge, so that sharing the stage with the extroverted Dame Edna brought out the best in him. For her part, Dame Edna whipped the crowd into a frenzy with her spirited go-go dancing. She had the hard-nosed ringers fighting for the gladiolis that she threw from the stage. To look at those blokes, with their dusty Akubras and freshly washed jeans, you would never guess they could be such flower lovers!

Dame Edna had meanwhile written an 'Ode to Slim' that she performed from the stage that night:

*Australia has hordes of superb vocal cords*
*Which time cannot silence or dim*
*But the larynx we love*
*All other above*
*The long, strong man they call Slim!*

Funds raised from the night went to the Royal Flying Doctor Service. The charity auction earlier in the night managed to shift some fairly strange things, including a

peacock and life-sized cut outs of Elle McPherson. One happy ringer was in fact last seen riding off into the sunset with his very own Elle!

Slim used this trip to one of the most spectacular scenic areas of Australia to shoot the cover for his new album *Ringer from the Top End*.

In the past Slim's covers had been fairly traditional studio head and shoulder type shots, but this time we would try for something else. I wanted to capture an image that reflected what Slim sang about, the Australian bush.

Early the next morning Slim and I joined the ringers from Carlton Hill Station as they went about a normal day's work. First up it was an exciting ride in a bull catcher, a ruggedly modified four-wheel drive that the ringers use to chase and catch bulls. I wedged myself between the bullbar and the radiator and shot back at Slim and the ringer as we sped along a bush track. Not only an exhilarating start to the day, but we got some good shots as well.

Next it was into the cattle yards where the boys were branding. The cattle had been kicking up dust and Slim was walking

**ABOVE** Slim, Dame Edna and Ernie Bridge wave farewell to the enthusiastic crowd

**RIGHT** 'We should be proud of this fine Kempsey boy,' Dame Edna gushed from the stage while performing her 'Ode to Slim'. This photograph was used by the National Portrait Gallery on their invitation to the opening of the gallery

**LEFT** 'This is the real Australia,' Slim claimed when he saw the concert site at Carlton Hill

**LEFT** With Richard Bradley in the bull catcher, which features in the song 'Old Yella Bull Catcher' on *Ringer from the Top End*

towards me with the cattle in the background. Slim looked at home in the dust so I clicked off a couple of shots. It would be one of these that would finally be the cover of *Ringer from the Top End*.

Slim stayed on at Carlton Hill to spend time in the bush camp on the Fitzroy River and do a spot of fishing. He also took the time to show a young Troy Cassar-Daley around the bush.

Slim and Troy struck up a friendship that has endured to this day, a friendship that would eventually produce a hit when Troy invited Slim to join him to record one of Slim's earlier hits, 'The Biggest Disappointment'.

# Field of Dreams

## 1993

Childhood memories came flooding back for Slim Dusty during Kempsey's Country Music Heritage Week in 1993. With me playing chauffeur, Slim slipped quietly out of town for a nostalgic visit to Nulla Nulla Creek — the place where it all began ...

**LEFT**  At the family farm at Nulla Nulla Creek. Slim and Joy were thrilled to be able to buy the property where Slim grew up

Slim Dusty and Joy McKean had originally intended to take a helicopter flight from Kempsey to Slim's old family farm, an hour's drive west. But at the last minute Slim suggested we drive. It seemed he needed the extra time to ready himself before he again walked the roads of the valley – the valley where some people still knew him as David Gordon Kirkpatrick.

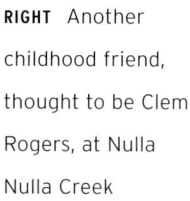
**ABOVE** Slim's childhood friend Shorty Ranger sitting outside the ruins of the dairy on the farm at Nulla Nulla in the late '40s

**RIGHT** Another childhood friend, thought to be Clem Rogers, at Nulla Nulla Creek

As we got closer to Nulla Nulla Creek, Slim reminisced about how his life – and the world – had changed in the fifty years since he left the sheltered valley on the Macleay River.

'I walked this road to school as a kid, and now I've spent a lifetime doing what I dreamed of doing. Today the valley seems so small ... there is so much bushland, so many trees. The stretches of country where I walked and rode as a child seemed so vast. It seems so different, so closed in. It's a hidden valley, a very beautiful hidden valley ...'

Slim's childhood memories have faded over the years, although he can still recall the times when his father would be laden down with lollies and chewing gum after one of his rare visits to town. Slim has a very clear perspective on his family history and where he fitted into the Kirkpatrick clan.

'George Kirkpatrick, my brother, was a great country kid. He became sick when he was nine years of age – they kept him too long in hospital. Dad eventually took him to Sydney but unfortunately he died of what they call sleeping meningitis. That really upset Dad and Mum.

'I'm here as a replacement ... I replaced my brother George. When I was young my parents really protected me – they were terrified something would happen to me. In lots of cases I wasn't allowed to do this and I wasn't allowed to do that.

'I was much younger than the other kids. The older ones got married – I was there with my Mum and Dad. That left me on my own ... in some ways that is why I started to sing.

'We had an old wind-up gramophone and I soon became fascinated by the old

*I walked this road to school as a kid, and now I've spent a lifetime doing what I dreamed of doing.*

American cowboy singers. From there I got interested in the poems of Henry Lawson and soon started singing. I eventually bought a guitar from the next door neighbour, Jack Kyle.'

It was during these childhood years that young David decided to adopt a new name – a name that would become synonymous with Australian country music.

'I called myself Slim Dusty when I was about ten years of age. I could see no future for David Kirkpatrick ... he was a country kid, he would never make it. From the moment I called myself Slim Dusty I definitely became another person and from that time I have always lived the feelings of that person I wanted to be. That's what drove me on.'

In some ways, that trip back to Nulla Nulla Creek was painful for Slim. He said that the memories of his dad and mum were with him in every room of the old homestead.

'Sitting in my old room all the feelings, doubts, hopes and dreams I had as a youngster came back ... Looking at the dining room I could remember the bush dances we had there – people came from miles. It was in this room that I first heard

country music performed live. A young Aboriginal lad sang the Jimmie Rodgers song, "A Drunkard's Child", and played slide guitar – I was fascinated.'

The years on the farm provided much of the inspiration for Slim's early songs.

'I remember sitting at the cow bails, getting the first thoughts for "When the Rain Tumbles Down in July". It was the story of a

**ABOVE** Childhood memories came flooding back when Slim stepped inside his old family home drover coming back home, but for some reason I finished the first verse with the line, "when the rain tumbles down in July" and I thought, "that sounds right", and soon the song evolved. I wrote the whole song in my head until I had it right and then committed it to paper at night after the work was done.'

When Slim originally left Kempsey for the bright lights of Sydney, there were many doubters – people who thought, 'That crazy Kirkpatrick kid will never make it'.

After fifty years of achieving more success than most people would ever dream of, Slim can look back and laugh at the delight he took on returning to his home town during the success of 'Pub With No Beer'.

'I had a flash new car and was on the road with Frank Foster, who we had a partnership with, touring the show grounds. When we got to Kempsey I parked my car in the middle of town and thought, "Well, I've made it".'

All those years down the road from that farm it was a more humble Slim on this trip back to Kempsey.

'I really appreciate the respect shown to me by the people of my home town. I enjoyed being in the parade and seeing lots of familiar faces from the old days.'

**BELOW** Sitting on the remains of the cow bails where he would sit each day when he was a boy. This is the exact spot where he wrote 'When the Rain Tumbles Down in July' in the late '40s

Slim had last visited the farm at Nulla Nulla Creek in 1979 while researching his book, *Walk a Country Mile*. Following that visit he wrote the song, 'The Day I Went Back Home'. It contained a rather poignant verse:

*Then I got that same old feeling*
*That I'd known so long ago*
*It said 'move on restless stranger*
*It's time for you to go'*
*With the strangest kind of mixture*
*Of happiness and pain*
*I knew then that I'd never come back*
*to the creek again*

Slim's life has continued to evolve, especially over the past decade. He appears comfortable with his place as the figurehead of country music in Australia and the memories of those uncertain childhood years seem to have mellowed.

On the drive back to Kempsey, Slim and Joy asked to stop so that they could walk across the Nulla Nulla Creek bridge. Slim had returned to the creek. As I watched him and Joy I knew that not only was I witnessing a special moment but also that somehow 'the creek' would always play a big part in their busy lives.

**ABOVE** Slim and Joy inspecting the plaque outside his childhood home

Early in 2001, Slim and Joy leapt at the chance to purchase the old family property when it went on the market.

'We are thrilled pink,' Slim said. 'The farm is bigger now – we have fifteen hundred acres in total. We have actually bought what was originally our farm, some of the country Dad used to lease and another property called Basin Flat which belonged to our neighbours, the Kyles.'

Slim and Joy plan to eventually refurbish the house and have it like it was when Slim and his family lived there.

In the future Slim and Joy would like to open the house to the public but first they have to take care of the elderly couple who are caretakers on the property and who are living in the house.

'The Kempsey council and community are working on getting funding for a museum and we would like to work with them,' Joy said.

'We have so much historical memorabilia and there is really no home for it. So much country music came from the north coast and it all needs to be remembered, not just Slim's music.'

*I called myself Slim Dusty when I was about ten years of age. I could see no future for David Kirkpatrick.*

**ABOVE**  Slim and Joy with some New Zealand fans on the drive back to town. The fans had driven to the valley to catch a glimple of Slim's childhood home

**LEFT**  With Bruce and Jo Rossiter, who once owned Slim's place at Nulla Nulla Creek near Kempsey

# Risky Business: Slim and Keith

## 1993

You couldn't get a more unusual combination than Slim Dusty and Keith Urban. Slim, the living legend of Australian country music, and Keith, former *Star Maker* winner who now lives in the USA, appear at first glance to be at different ends of the musical spectrum. But when Slim invited Keith to join him on the Slim Dusty Tour in November 1993, there wasn't a moment's hesitation from the young singer-songwriter.

**LEFT** Keith Urban and Slim Dusty with a big rig in Moree, western New South Wales

At the time, this move certainly raised eyebrows among some of the country music fraternity. After all, Keith had added back-up vocals to a recent INXS album, and appeared to have forsaken the sunburnt country for a life of glitz and glamour in North America. And on Slim's side, his general avoidance of risk taking as against the tried and true was well known. (Admittedly, Slim had tried something different in the '70s when he signed up the Hamilton County Bluegrass Band to join his touring roadshow, and that had worked.)

But then, as now, Slim knew what he was doing. 'I met Keith when he was a youngster in Tamworth in the late '70s. I watched his talent grow and his career take off,' he said. 'I like what he does and I'm saying to my older fans, have a listen and see what you think. I guess I took a risk, but it worked.'

In support of Slim's opinion, Keith had the right credentials. As well as the *Star Maker* award, he had won the Golden Guitar for Best New Talent at Tamworth in 1991, followed by Male Vocalist of the Year in 1992.

So away they went. First stop was Moree, and Slim, Joy and Heather McKean had the crowd hopping during the first half of the show. It was during the second half that Slim introduced his wild card. Although it was a comparatively subdued Keith Urban performance, the crowd warmed to his music.

**BELOW** Keith Urban on stage at the sound check. Keith had just heard how loud Slim has his on-stage sound monitors. Jimmy Barnes is the only Australian musician who has his on-stage monitors louder than Slim!

As the tour progressed, Keith became part of the 'family'. His performances, solo and in combination with Slim, especially on 'Lights on the Hill', were well received and the concert-goers reacted enthusiastically.

The response pleased Slim.

'The fans really accepted Keith and me together. I like some of the ballads he does and I love his guitar playing, especially the short tribute he does to Barry Thornton on "Winter Winds".'

The tour wound its way through New South Wales, Victoria and South Australia. Six weeks, thousands of kilometres and thirty concerts later, the successful experi-ment drew to an end at Albury  with the final concert on 20 December.  It was an experience that will long remain in the memory of young Keith.

'The opportunity to tour with Slim was a once in a lifetime thing. It gave me the chance to see parts of Australia I've never seen before and the chance to reach a lot of people who wouldn't normally come to one of my shows. It was just great – even the older people seemed to like my music.'

Years later, of course, Keith was to repay Slim for taking him on the road when Keith and his band backed Slim at the Grand Ole Opry in Nashville.

**ABOVE**  Keith Urban and Joy McKean swapping song-writing ideas

In 2001 Keith also surprised Slim and Joy when he made a special appearance at the Slim Dusty Chairman's Dinner in Tamworth. This dinner was a get-together for about a hundred of Slim's mates. Keith's performance was basically an acoustic set – no band, no stage and only a small sound system. Just

*Slim and Joy looked like proud parents as they watched and listened to this young Australian.*

Keith and his guitar on the floor and right next to Slim and Joy's table.

Keith decided at the last minute – actually, in the shower before his performance – to perform a slow, bluesy version of Slim's 'Lights on the Hill', which was written by Joy McKean. He didn't get a chance to rehearse his radical new arrangement of this iconic song but Keith's performance that night was magic.

Slim and Joy looked like proud parents as they watched and listened to this young Australian who, since touring through the Australian bush as a member of the Slim Dusty Show, has gone on to achieve major international success.

**ABOVE** Keith on stage with Slim and the McKean Sisters for the finale, a rollicking version of 'Lights on the Hill'

**LEFT** Keith and Slim chatting about the tour

# Slim and his Mates

## 1996

Back in the '40s, on a remote dairy farm in the hills behind Kempsey, a ten-year-old boy dreamed of being a country music singer. He called himself 'Slim Dusty' and, as he's said himself, began to 'live that dream'. But even the most optimistic farm boy would never have imagined the life that was to unfold, a life that would establish Slim as the voice of our nation, the chronicler of over half a century of Australia's history.

**LEFT**  With the Screaming Jets. Slim and Dave Gleason of the Jets became friends after the band recorded Slim's song 'Cunnamulla Fella'. Dave credits Slim with giving him the courage to sing with an Aussie accent

More than fifty years on, the dream is brighter than ever. The main reason Slim Dusty has managed to hold on to those early visions of writing and singing about the bush is that during his lengthy career he has kept in touch with his audience. He has managed to do this in a very real and meaningful way, so much so that most fans would feel that Slim is one of their mates and his songs just a good yarn you might hear from a mate at the pub, around a camp fire in the bush or at a backyard barbie. Slim describes his music as 'songs about real Australians'.

'I have to be fair dinkum with my audience. I can't see any other way of doing it. You have to believe in what you are singing about!'

A few years back, Slim was included in a list of 'national treasures' by the *Good Weekend* magazine, on the occasion of that magazine's tenth birthday. The magazine

> *Most fans would feel that Slim is one of their mates and his songs just a good yarn you might hear from a mate at the pub.*

says of the people featured, 'These are people of talent and courage, fortitude and vision, people who are integral to the pride we feel in our country. Their accomplishments are part of who we are'. Qualities that all apply to Slim Dusty.

Slim believes the reason for his continuing popularity is simple.

'The secret is to meet the people, talk with them, in some cases live with them, and then sing songs about them, about fair dinkum Australians. All my songs are about them. I'm just as proud to be an Australian as the next man and I want my audience to feel the same way.'

One of the ways Slim has stayed in touch with his audience and with the real world is to have always stayed in touch with his friends. Slim's mates have always been there as a sounding board for him. And if you are a friend of Slim's it's not unusual to get a phone call at any time of the day or night, occasions when he will call for a chat or seeking advice.

Let's hear from some of Slim's mates:

## ROD COE

Slim's long-time record producer and bass player in the Travelling Country Band

'Back in the mid '70s I was on staff at EMI and Slim's previous producer Peter Dawkins left to go to Festival. I had already been working with The Hamilton County Bluegrass Band in the studio so I sort of inherited the job to produce Slim. Slim said I was "trainable" so I got the position.

'I can remember the first album I worked on with Slim – it was *Things I See Around Me*. I was on tenterhooks, there was such a big age difference between Slim and me, but I was confident I could do the job.

'Slim's biggest strength is that he knows what works for him and he is prepared to give new things a go. He won't stop and I can't see him slowing down. He is still alert and on the ball, has incredible drive and he really likes the travelling life. He will continue to tour because Slim thrives on audience feedback, it is his lifeblood.

'Even now Slim will follow his instincts. When Keith Urban recorded "Lights on the Hill" he asked Slim if he would join him on the vocal. Slim didn't hesitate, he had faith that it would work for him.

'Slim has a couple of unusual habits. He likes recording early in the day. Over the years we have had a bit of trouble getting engineers and musicians into the studio at 9 am. I remember once we were trying a new drummer in the studio and on the second day he was late. That was the end of that.

'Slim has a rather unusual habit before going on stage. He carries a small pair of blue-handled scissors with him on tour and every night he goes through the ritual of cutting up throat lozenges and putting them in his shirt pocket. Through the night he has a constant supply of small throat lollies to help his voice through the concert.

'Slim is probably the most self-contained entertainer I know. He writes or selects the songs, knows how he wants them to sound and is a unique singer. He knows it all.'

**ABOVE** Rod Coe and Slim discussing the night's concert

## DAVID BAXTER

Former strategic marketing director for EMI

'I was state promotions manager with EMI when I had my first contact with Slim. I worked with him on the promotion of *Walk a Country Mile* but I was obviously aware of Slim well before that. I feel that I have grown up with Slim. We worked closely together when 'Duncan' went to number one.

'Slim is a real Australian icon, just like Vegemite. He is incredibly successful but still unaffected and down to earth.

'I came back to EMI in 1988 to work with him before Bill Robertson retired. I worked with Rod Coe in the A & R area with Slim and looked after artwork, videos and marketing concepts for Slim's product. Even though he has sold five million records, he is still your mate. I am happy to say that I feel part of the Slim Dusty "family".'

## BILL ROBERTSON

Former consultant to EMI

'I started work at EMI in 1947, the same time as Slim, but it wasn't until the '60s that I really got acquainted with him. In 1980 I was called in by the managing director and told I would be working with Slim on a day-to-day basis.

'Slim goes back to the era when simple songs were the go. He sings about Australia but not too many love songs. With his clear diction you can hear every word.

'Like many great artists Slim can be a bit temperamental and over the years we have had our little tiffs, but with Slim it is over the next day. Over the years we all became one big happy family.

'I don't think Slim will ever stop working, although he has had more retirements than Nellie Melba. Slim would become bored if he wasn't working. While the people love him why shouldn't he keep giving them his music? Believe me, the fans do love him!

'One of my major jobs at EMI was organising Slim's extensive back catalogue. Prior to me doing the job some uninformed, moronic twit had a clean-out at EMI and chucked out a lot of the old Slim Dusty master tapes. This was before 1960. Fortunately over the years we have managed to find copies of these historic Slim Dusty recordings. Collectors from around Australia have allowed us to make copies. I know where to find most of the Slim Dusty catalogue.

'I left EMI in August 1993 because I thought it was time, but still do part-time work for them. Slim and I talk often and we go fishing occasionally.'

**RIGHT** Slim with David Baxter

## TONY BROOKS

Songwriter and long-time mate of Slim's. Slim has recorded sixteen of Tony's songs including 'Jimberella Kid' and 'When the Scrubbers Break'

'I remember going to see Slim in Mount Isa at the AWU Hall and before that at a church hall on mineside in the early '60s.

'I used to write poetry and one night when we were all drunk I offered to write a song for one of my cab driver mates. The first one I ever wrote was "When the Scrubbers Break". I put it in an envelope and addressed it to Slim Dusty, care of the Mount Isa Post Office. Eight months later I got a letter from Slim saying that he had recorded it and did I have any more. And, being a brash young man, I said, "Of course, I've got thousands of them". I sat down and wrote a heap of them. It taught me a lesson because only one of them got recorded, that was "Roughriders".

*I don't think Slim will ever stop working, although he has had more retirements than Nellie Melba.*

'From then on I was more selective. When I eventually got a copy of the record with "When the Scrubbers Break" on it I nearly wore the bloody thing out.

'I remember the first time I met Slim. I was standing in a Mount Isa street after an AWU meeting and bugger me dead if Slim didn't pull up and ask me directions to the Breakaway Caravan Park. The next year when he was in town I went up and had a yarn with him at his motel.

'Slim's personality hasn't changed over the years although his music has changed with the times. Most of his old fans don't agree with some of the changes but on the whole he is still as relevant as ever.

'I write lots of songs and still give Slim first whack at them. For a long time I didn't think I could write on demand. Slim wanted to write a song about the Kokoda Track and ran out of time. He asked me if I'd do it and I managed to come up with a good song. It's one of Slim's more dramatic songs. "My Time" was another song of mine that Slim recorded and did a different treatment on. To this day I've never heard "My Time" played on the radio.

'Joy and Slim are terribly rapt in their music. Slim will play and sing all bloody day and night. Slim also loves his fishing. He likes to get on a waterhole with no one else around.'

**LEFT**  'I'm just as proud to be an Australian as the next man and I want my audience to feel the same way,' says Slim

# It's Dusty in Nashville

## 1998

Slim Dusty has had an abundance of career highlights. On Friday, 15 August 1998 he notched up another one. This was the day Slim played the Grand Ole Opry in Nashville, USA. The invitation to perform in the heart of US country music, and at one of its great institutions, came in recognition of Slim's outstanding contribution to Australian country music.

**LEFT** Slim and his trusty Maton guitar on stage at the Grand Ole Opry

Slim slotted the American trip into his busy touring schedule and called up his mate Keith Urban, who is now a Nashville resident. Slim invited Urban and his band The Ranch to back him at the Opry performance, and the young Australian was thrilled.

'I had always hoped I would get to play the Grand Ole Opry, but had started to think that because of the rock influences in my music, I might not get asked,' Urban said. 'To play the Opry with one of the greats – Slim – was a double whammy.'

Slim and his pickup band for the Opry performance had one rehearsal for the big night. It was at the home of a friend of Lawrie Minson's, just off Music Row, the music business centre of Nashville. Even though Keith's band knew the songs intimately Slim went through the repertoire

several times. He wasn't nervous about working with a new band, but he did want to get it right and fulfil his self-imposed obligation to deliver his very best to the audience. The rehearsal went well and Slim and the boys from The Ranch and Lawrie spent most of the afternoon yarning on the front porch of the beautiful old home.

While in Nashville Slim and Joy took the opportunity to catch up with their good friend James Blundell who, like Keith Urban, was also living in that city. At the time, James was writing material for a new album, *Amsterdam Breakfast*, one that would change his career direction when released in Australia a couple of years later. James took Slim and Joy for a tour of Nashville in his monster American car.

The night before Slim's performance at the Grand Ole Opry I joined Slim and Joy for dinner at their hotel, The Opryland

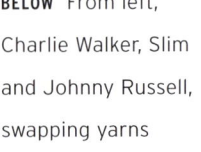

**BELOW** From left, Charlie Walker, Slim and Johnny Russell, swapping yarns

Hotel. The hotel is so big they hand you a map at the reception desk so that you are sure to find the room you are looking for. Although my navigation skills aren't the best, I eventually tracked down Slim and Joy in their room. It was good to see them again. The first thing Slim did was reach into his suitcase and produce a tape player to let me listen to songs for his next album, one that he had recorded just before leaving Australia.

Slim and Joy's room overlooked the most amazing artificial lagoon in the atrium of the hotel and Slim said, 'You have arrived just in time for the evening's performance. We were sitting in our room at this time last night minding our own business when next minute I hear the loudest piano I have ever heard. You won't believe this.'

We sat on the balcony outside their room and watched as the lagoon transformed into a ballet of water, with brightly lit fountains of water suddenly shooting into the air. All of this to accompany the over-the-top piano-playing of a Liberace-type character who had magically appeared (with a grand piano) from out of the water. It was American schmaltz and glitz at its best or worst, depending on how you were feeling at the time. (You were right Slim, I didn't believe it.)

**ABOVE** The Ranch – Gerry Flowers, Keith Urban and Peter Clarke – with Lawrie Minson and Slim getting in a little rehearsal before the show

**TOP RIGHT** Backstage after the Opry show. From left, Slim, Joy, Lawrie Minson, Peter Clarke, Keith Urban, Gerry Flowers, John McSweeney, James Blundell and Jeff Walker

The night was young and already I was feeling pretty weird. One moment I'm lost in my own little world, listening to the music of Slim Dusty through headphones, eyes shut, engrossed in Slim's new songs and momentarily back in Australia – Slim's unique voice and his music have me in the Australian outback, I can see it, feel it, I can smell the dust.

Next minute my senses are being bombarded by a crazed piano player in a strange and surreal setting in the biggest

## Slim and the boys kicked in and the crowd, which contained every Australian living in Nashville, loved it.

**BOTTOM RIGHT** Slim and the band running through the songs

hotel in the world. It is almost too much for this boy from Blackall to handle and in the middle of all of this cultural mayhem is Slim Dusty, as cool as a cucumber.

The next night was to be Slim's big night. The Grand Ole Opry is famous the world over on the country music scene. It started out as a radio broadcast on Nashville radio station WSM on 28 November 1925, and soon grew into a regular Friday and Saturday live concert as well as the radio show. Home for the Opry from 1943 until 1974 was the Ryman Auditorium in downtown Nashville. In 1974 it moved to the Grand Ole Opry House, a four thousand-seat auditorium that would become the centrepiece of the Opryland Theme Park.

I arrived at the Opry early to make sure I had accreditation so that I could photograph Slim's performance. I found my way to the backstage entrance and chatted with the lady at the entrance. She is a good ol' southern gal.

'Hi, my name's John Elliott and I'm here to photograph the Slim Dusty performance.'

She scannned her list, found my name and invited me in. I was amazed at the informality of the process, having experienced the backstage nazi behaviour at some Australian concerts where you are forced to wear dog-tag style identification badges.

When I enquired if I needed to wear any ID she replied in her southern drawl, 'Darlin' once you get past me you can do whatever you want.' I guess this comes with the familiarity of doing regular shows at only two different venues for almost fifty years.

The line-up for the night of Slim's performance was impressive – Grandpa Jones, Charlie Louvin, Porter Wagoner, George Hamilton IV, Jack Greene, Johnny Russell, Jeannie Seely, Ricky Skaggs, Del Reeves, Stonewall Jackson and Tommy Overstreet. Slim and The Ranch were joined by fellow Australian Lawrie Minson, who played dobro and didgeridoo. Slim was in fine form and intrigued the American crowd with his patter to introduce 'Ringer from the Top End'.

'A ringer is like one of your cowboys, and where I wrote this song, the paddocks are a couple of million acres each, and crocodiles eat a few head of cattle each day.'

Slim and the boys kicked in and the crowd, which contained every Australian living in Nashville, loved it. It was one of the

few times I had ever seen Slim on stage without the Travelling Country Band. 'Ringer from the Top End', 'Pub With No Beer', and 'Lights on the Hill' had them screaming for more. The crowd might not have heard too many Aussie bush ballads before, but that didn't dampen their enthusiasm.

One American, who was already a big fan of Slim, happened to be another of the performers on the bill, Texan Charlie Walker.

'I come out of the old school of country music and love Slim's music – that's real country music,' Walker said. ' "Pub With No Beer" is one of my all time favorites. I am just delighted that Slim has made it to the Grand

*It is almost too much for this boy from Blackall to handle and in the middle of all of this cultural mayhem is Slim Dusty, as cool as a cucumber.*

Ole Opry. I really enjoyed meeting him after all these years. It was a great thrill.'

Although there are four thousand people in the audience, the Opry is very much a casual night out. It is almost like sitting in someone's lounge room and listening to your mates sing. Once you have entrance to the backstage area you can actually go and sit on stage to watch the performers. There are a couple of rows of seats on stage, immediately

**RIGHT** Slim and the elegantly attired Porter Wagoner

**RIGHT** Two country music veterans – Slim with Grandpa Jones

**LEFT** Jack Green and Slim

behind the band. It is a great spot to watch the show from but it must be disconcerting for the performers to know that there are twenty people staring at the backs of their heads.

Backstage at the Opry that night Slim asked me to do him a favour. I noticed that he was taking extra care packing his custom-built Maton guitar into its case. He clipped the lid of the case shut, looked up at me and asked, 'John, would you mind taking this back to Australia for me?' (Turned out that following the Opry performance Slim and Joy were going to spend time holidaying in America.) Of course I immediately said 'yes', but then the doubts started to set in. I thought, 'Shit, what happens if I lose Slim's guitar?'

It was with some trepidation that I checked Slim's guitar through with the rest of my luggage for the flight back to Australia. I am pleased to report that the Maton survived the flight from Nashville to Memphis to Chicago on to Los Angeles and back to Sydney. I finally breathed a big sigh of relief when I personally delivered the guitar to its owner when he returned to Australia four weeks later.

Although the US had never been a part of Slim's career path, he was delighted to have performed at the Grand Ole Opry and was appreciative of the applause from the fans and the warm welcome from the other performers. After giving the mainly American audience such a positive lesson in 'down under' culture, it seems that there may be a market for real Australian music in the home of American country music after all.

# One More for the Road

## 1998

It may be a long way to the top if you want to rock and roll, but try climbing into Slim Dusty's well-worn R.M. Williams boots. Despite a gruelling touring schedule that began in the early '50s, Slim has remained a prolific musician. It's a commitment that's continued throughout his career.

**LEFT**  Slim in the late '50s with his pride and joy – a '57 Ford Customline. This was the first automatic transmission model available in Australia

Since the beginning, Slim has taken his music on the road, putting together an annual show and touring it extensively. For many of those kilometres Slim was behind the wheel driving the trucks from show to show. While Slim himself doesn't travel by truck much these days, his association with the trucking industry has lasted a lifetime. It's been the inspiration for many of his songs and a happy memory of life on the road that hasn't faded with time. I caught up with him on tour in Kingaroy, Queensland, to find out what it was like all those years ago.

'My first tour was in '54,' Slim recalled. 'From Sydney to Toowoomba and back. We had a '38 Ford and a caravan with a great big tow bar on it. The caravan took four of us to pick up and we'd put it on the back of that poor old Ford and she'd just about lift off the ground.'

The first tour hit the road with wife Joy, daughter Anne, and Larry Mason and Barry Thornton. In those early days accommodation usually took the form of camping outside the halls where they performed, with some of the crew bunking down in the dressing rooms.

'I remember on that trip it was quite wet,' Slim went on. 'We had to cross the river below Taree and the water was up over the low bridge. Even today when we're travelling we look for those old bridges … most people wouldn't even know where they were.'

The Slim Dusty Touring Show grew and eventually needed a couple of trucks to move it around the country efficiently. Slim had two Internationals – the big one was affectionately called Old Thunder and the small one was called Lightning.

'Boy, oh boy! They were good trucks. During one of our trips we put a hole through the side of the motor and all we had

RIGHT  Camped by the roadside near Collarenebri, western New South Wales, in 1955

was self-tapping screws and Bostick. Those self-tappers were still in the side of the block when we sold the trucks.'

With a couple of trucks to haul his show to town, Slim could now attempt larger and longer tours and in the late '60s the bush troubadour took the tour across the Nullarbor to Western Australia. At the time, the Eyre Highway across the Nullarbor was still ninety per cent corrugations and a hundred per cent bulldust. And the touring party included the two trucks, as well as four caravans to help slow down the proceedings even further.

'It would take three to four days to get across,' Slim recalls. 'I remember one trip – there were big signs up that said 'BEWARE OF BULLDUST HOLES'. It was like talcum powder. If you went into them too fast it would spray up over the car and you would have to put your windscreen wipers on to clean it ... there was about seven hundred and fifty miles of dirt.'

Back in those days Slim and his family would have a break at Metung in Victoria over the Christmas period before heading off on the road again.

Barry Thornton and Slim were the truck drivers most of the time. They carried their own spares and while on the road they kept the trucks well serviced, oiled and greased. The vehicles were hosed down once a week and the cabs kept tidy.

'We felt if we kept them clean and tidy we would be more particular about the mechanical side as well ... it seemed to work. We never had many breakdowns or holdups because we were prepared,' Slim recalled.

'We were only ever held up twice on the track; once at Rowena, a little town south of Walgett with no pub ... fancy being stuck for four days in a town with no pub ... Another time we got stuck on a stretch up the top of Western Australia at a place called the Mardie Plains ... a big boggy flat below Roebourne; there were trucks, tourists and caravans stuck with us and luckily for them we always carried supplies of fruit juices, tinned meats and things under the bunks in the caravans. We ended up supplying a lot of people with a bit of tucker.'

Slim and his show fly across the Nullarbor these days but in 1997 he once

**ABOVE** Slim and Barry Thornton digging out the vehicle after becoming bogged in a bore drain

*During one of our trips we put a hole through the side of the motor and all we had was self-tapping screws and Bostick.*

again made the crossing by road, this time in a Thompson's Transport road train.

'Compared with the old days of dust and dirt, crossing the Nullarbor in an air-conditioned road train on the bitumen was a breeze.'

Slim and Joy have always felt close to truckies. 'We had a lot in common with the truck drivers in those early days. Just like the truckies, we had to really watch ourselves. Some of those roads were pretty isolated in the mid to late '60s, the truck stops were at the old time stations. They were pretty wild and woolly places.'

Slim remembers one of the trips across the Nullarbor that tested their ingenuity.

'We took our show across on the train and drove back in my Ford Ranchwagon pulling a big twenty-five foot caravan with

*We were our own bosses and we treasured Sunday nights when we'd pull our vans way off the road and park them in a circle.*

bogey wheels. The bloody Ranchwagon snapped its chassis. We made it through to the old Cocklebiddy which the McDonald family owned. They'd stopped there years ago when they were going across the Nullarbor on the Show run. People stopped to get cups of tea off them and they eventually set up a building and it became one of the first roadhouses in that part of the world.'

'They couldn't do much with the Ranchwagon so we got saplings and wired the chassis together until we got across to the eastern side of the Nullarbor.'

The constant travelling may have seemed tedious to some people but Slim claims those times hold a fond place in his memory.

'We travelled about forty thousand miles over eight to ten months around Australia every year, year after year. We had our own advance agent ahead of us. He'd ring us once a week and we'd go to a post office and wait for his call.

'We were our own bosses and we treasured Sunday nights when we'd pull our vans way off the road and park them in a circle. That was our night to howl.

'One of these camps I remember well,' Slim recalled. 'We were about eighty or ninety miles out of Norseman and we'd pulled off the road to have our night off. We had a good time, a barbecue and a few beers. The next afternoon in Norseman one of the blokes on our tour said, "I can't find my wallet, it must have fallen out when I was lounging around the fire last night".

'We couldn't go back because we had a two-and-a-half month tour ahead of us. Well, we did our tour and on the way back we camped at the same spot. We drove to the spot and the coals from our camp fire were still there and right next to them was the wallet. The money was a bit tatty but it was still there.

'While we swallowed a lot of dust, we were free, we breathed fresh air,' Slim says with a hint of nostalgia. 'Our vehicles weren't air-conditioned and then all of a sudden we were in air-conditioned cars, planes and

motels. I still reckon our old rough life was healthier than what we do today.'

Over time progress caught up with the Slim Dusty Touring Show. With Slim's growing popularity the day finally arrived when people wanted Slim in all parts of Australia at the same time. Not only had the Slim Dusty Show itself grown over the years, the advent of television meant people expected a bigger production with lights and sound systems.

Eventually Slim had to employ a production crew with a truck. The days of travelling by basic truck and caravan were over. From having just a few people on the road Slim now travels with a crew of about eighteen.

'We have a pretty regular sound crew; they come from Canberra. They're just as important as the band. It doesn't matter how good the band is, you still need good sound equipment and operators,' explains Slim.

'I like being on the road – it's similar to the trucking scene. You really have to balance every day, nothing is done haphazardly, everything has got to be planned. Wheels are what get us there and keep us moving, just like the trucking scene.'

John McFarlane was the production manager on the Slim Dusty Touring Show for many years; his main truck was a Hino FD 22' pantech.

'We're pretty compact,' John explained. 'All up we carry nine or ten tonnes on the road. We used to carry tonnes and tonnes of gear and we still carry a heap but it's now more efficient in how it's utilised.'

Like most delivery jobs, John reckons now and then they'll get to a venue that's difficult to get the gear into.

'If they can stick a theatre on the top floor they will. We've backed up to a loading dock, loaded into a lift, and then had a sixty or seventy metre push and then had to lift the

**ABOVE** On the road near Narrabri, western New South Wales. From left, Johnny Ashcroft, Bob McKean holding Anne, and Slim

**ABOVE** In the north-west of Australia in the '60s. Rocky Page is sitting in the truck chatting to a visitor

gear up onto a stage. It's a bonus when we get to a venue that's easy to load into.

A day off, or a day with only a hundred and fifty kilometres to travel is a real luxury but when you have three or four hundred kilometres of winding and hilly roads with an average speed of 80 kph, that takes its toll on the truck and crew.'

Of necessity, Slim and his team need a truck that's absolutely reliable, as the consequences of not getting to a gig with the lighting and stage equipment can be catastrophic. Especially when there's more than a thousand Slim fans at the front door waiting for the show to start.

'In the twelve years of doing this I've never had a problem getting to a gig,' John said while touching wood. And just to make sure any problem can be taken care of on the spot he has tickets in rigging, electrical safety, first aid and a truck-driving licence.

John says problems crop up all the time and, in the great entertainment industry tradition, the show must go on.

'It's a pressure job,' he says of his work. 'There is no room for error, and it has to be perfect first time. In the studio you can spend all week getting the right sound, but when you have a thousand screaming fans expecting CD-quality sound at the concert you have basically about thirty seconds to get it perfect. It can be demanding and you learn to fly by the seat of your pants very quickly. Once you've got it right, things normally stay pretty stable.'

Finally, Slim's experiences of the touring life were gained over many years and thousands of kilometres. Here are some of his impressions and recollections:

## ON DRIVING

'We always changed drivers at least every two hours or so to keep fresh. Just don't sit there until you're starry-eyed. It's funny how they emphasise that on the roads now.

'I can remember driving in the old days. Sometimes you would have to drive until the late afternoon going onto the night and you'd see horses and cattle that weren't there. When we started there wasn't the traffic on the road that there is now. It's very crazy to drive when you're tired.

'Joy didn't drive in the beginning but, soon after, she started to drive and pull a caravan. I drove one of the trucks for a long time. I drove Thunder and Barry drove Lightning and then we'd switch. We never had many breakdowns or big disasters because we looked after our vehicles.

'We had a great mate with a garage in East Gippsland who was used to fixing tractors and all the odd jobs for the farmers so both our old trucks would go in there and he would really work on them when we had the layoff over the Christmas period. The vehicles were pretty solid when we left. Prevention was always the number one word.'

## ON TRAVELLING

'You get to know the places. We do carry what we call a 'kitchen suitcase' so that we can make a meal for ourselves. You have to. We watch our meals and diet pretty well. We aren't fanatical but we like to eat good food.

'For years we have carried a little red teapot on the road. We even took it to England. We played at the Mean Fiddler just out of London and Rolf Harris came to the show and came around the back to say hello. I had my little red teapot and was pouring myself a cup of tea and Rolf nearly fell over. Apparently he travels with a red teapot too.

'On tour we have at least one night off a week. It gives you a good break. Normally Joy, Anne and I and some of the boys have a nice meal together. We never tire of each other's company because each member of the band has their own personality and we all lead a pretty quiet life and we all enjoy the break.'

## ON WORKING WITH HIS TEAM

'It is almost as if we have one mind sometimes. I know what Joy's thinking without either of us saying a word. I've got a saying – nobody does things entirely their own. I'm a great believer that you do it as a team, so Joy and I work as a team. Joy and I work with our band as a team, and Arthur Laing, our promoter joins us, and then he joins the team. So we're all a big team.

'Rod Coe, my producer, bass player and bandleader, he controls the band. Joy and I work together on songs – not so much on composing songs – we sort of work out what songs we'll use in the show. We work in with the road crew. If we have a good road crew, we try to keep them with us for a long time. We are pretty fair and we get a fair deal back. The old roadie's job is a pretty hard one. We have a chap called Wayne, he's been with us on and off for years. Wayne is a great character. It's always the standard joke when something goes wrong – everyone says, "Do

*I had my little red teapot and was pouring myself a cup of tea and Rolf nearly fell over. Apparently he travels with a red teapot too.*

something Wayne". No matter how much trouble he's in, Wayne is always smiling!'

Slim has the last word: 'The young ones who tour today and complain about their room because it mightn't have enough light in it or the carpet doesn't look right, they don't know they're alive.'

It certainly is a long way to the top …

# On the Nullarbor

## 1998

The uniqueness of the Australian truck industry has always been an attraction for Slim Dusty. His interest in the trucking world can be traced to the many years Slim and his wife Joy spent working on the show grounds.

**LEFT** Keith Thompson, Bev Brown, Slim, Carol Thompson, Joy McKean and Noel Brown, standing in front of the Kenworths, ready to cross the Nullarbor

'Truck drivers are like show people,' Slim says, 'and we have spent a lot of time on the show grounds over the years. We feel that we have something in common with the showies and the truck drivers. If you're not in the game you're an outsider, and that's the attitude of a lot of truckies. There is a great bond, a great brotherhood – they all stick together.'

When Slim decided to do another truckin' album he spread the word to his team of songwriters and the songs started to pour in. But collecting material for his ninety-third album – *Makin' a Mile* – wasn't enough for Slim. Before the recording sessions had started, he wanted to be in the right frame of mind, and that meant taking a road-train trip across the Nullarbor from Adelaide to Perth.

Slim called and invited me on the trip. Slim has a good nose for a story and he knew that this unpublicised trip would give me

plenty of photo opportunities. Besides which, the trip would also be a whole lot of fun and Slim likes having his mates along if there are good times to be had.

It isn't all that easy to arrange travel on a road train. It's not the sort of travel request that one can take to a local travel agent. However, a quick call to an old mate, Noel Brown, national sales manager of Re-Car Consolidated Industries, soon had the ball rolling. Slim and his wife are patrons of the Re-Car Truck Drivers Memorial at Tarcutta. Brown contacted Keith Thompson, of Thompson's Transport, Castlemaine, Victoria, who agreed to provide the trucks. The trip was on. Thompson phoned around his major customers and ended up with two trailers of Colgate Palmolive freight and two trailers of Bridgestone tires.

The itinerary was a rather leisurely six days with overnight stops at Port Augusta, Ceduna, Eucla, Balladonia, Kalgoorlie and finally delivering the load into Perth. Executive privilege was used in selecting drivers for the trip. Thompson decided he should drive one of the Kenworths and Brown volunteered to make a comeback as an interstater and drive the other one. The wives weren't going to be left home either. Bev Brown and Carol Thompson would drive the back-up vehicle.

The short haul to Port Augusta was all it took to start Slim reminiscing.

'This is just like the old days,' he said. 'It reminds me of back in the '60s when we would head off across to Perth early in the year with our big road show. The roads were dusty and as rough as guts, the trip would just about destroy our old Internationals. It's

**BELOW** A local oyster farmer showing Joy and Slim around Ceduna

a bloody lot more comfortable riding high in the Kenworth.'

Each day Slim and Joy would travel in the Kenworths, experiencing life in the big rigs.

'The trip has given me a whole new insight into how it is from the truck drivers perspective,' Joy said. 'I'm sure I'll get some good songs from it. When I'm writing I want to know how things work, and I love travelling, so this trip is giving me the best of both worlds.'

The next stop was Ceduna where a quick visit to one of the thriving oyster farms had been arranged, followed by a delicious dinner of local seafood. Truck-driving tours – this could really catch on!

Because the trip had purposely been kept low key, with no advance publicity, Slim enjoyed the chance to be just one of the boys. The further west we travelled, the easier it became. Truck drivers welcomed him as one of their own and swapped yarns about their work. Many commented on how well Slim looked. 'I hope I'm going as well as you when I'm your age,' said one.

After stopping for photographs with the quarantine inspectors on the Western Australian border, it was on to Eucla. The local police had arranged a late afternoon

*He wanted to be in the right frame of mind, and that meant taking a road train trip across the Nullarbor from Adelaide to Perth.*

tour of the scenic delights of the area. First Class Constable Phil Kuhne had the job of driving Slim across the sand dune covered site of old Eucla and then along a beautiful twenty kilometre section of beach. The trip was enjoyable, despite Kuhne bogging the four wheel drive on the return trip!

A quick moonlight drive around Eucla's new golf course, including chasing 'roos along the eighteenth, and the crew were back in time for a delightful dinner at the Eucla Motor Inn. On the way into the dining room, Slim said, 'I think I'll have a quiet one tonight so when I have finished dinner it's out the back door and into my room.'

Slim changed his mind and not surprisingly ended up in the bar. The man loves a beer but during his busy touring schedule he doesn't get time to party with the boys. Normally it's finish a concert, meet the fans, pack up his gear, back to the motel and maybe one or two stubbies with the band, then getting to bed ready for an early start the next day and several hours of driving to the next concert. This routine can go on day after day for up to six weeks at a time.

In Ceduna there was to be no concert the following night, so Slim took advantage of being with a couple of his mates and a bunch of party-loving locals at a bar in the outback. This was a night for yarn-spinning, research for future Slim Dusty songs, and enough drinking to leave the bar fresh out of Bundaberg rum by 11 pm.

The locals had taken the liberty early in the evening to warn Slim about one particularly argumentative local woman. They told him if she turned up at the bar she would definitely start an argument and the only

thing to do was tell her to bugger off. I had been keeping an eye on Slim in the crowded bar, making sure he didn't get into too much trouble. I spotted Slim at the end of the bar – a woman had him blocked in the corner and even from across the room I could tell that they were having something more than a chat. Edging closer I could hear their conversation.

'You are always sucking up to the black fellas,' the woman said.

'Half my mates are Aboriginal so I don't have to suck up to them,' Slim replied in a remarkably coherent state. 'I probably wouldn't have had a career without all my Aboriginal fans,' Slim was trying to rationalise.

The woman wouldn't have any of Slim's reasoning so he looked her straight in the eye and said, 'Why don't you bugger off!'. It was only then that I realised who the agitated woman was. She was the one stirrer the locals had warned Slim about.

It was getting late and eventually the locals left. The crowd had dwindled to just

**ABOVE** Getting ready for the long haul across the Nullarbor

**LEFT** Slim behind the wheel of the Kenworth

**ABOVE** The local
police at Ceduna
dropped in for a chat
with Slim before
inviting him back to
the station to sign
their wall

the barman, Slim, Noel and Keith and the barman had had enough. He said, 'Bugger you blokes, I'm off to bed.'

It was only then that the trio decided to call it quits. It seemed like a simple process — all I had to do was get the three of them back to their motel rooms and the motel was right next door. Surely it couldn't be all that difficult.

How wrong can you be?

As the three of them had a bellyful of booze, the gravel driveway to the motel was proving to be a little difficult for my mates. Maintaining any dignity while trying to walk along that drive was seriously beyond them. The motel was in darkness, the rest of the guests were sleeping and my mates were getting progressively louder.

The thought crossed my mind that if the manager of the motel chucked us out we probably wouldn't get another bed in Eucla at one in the morning. To top things off Slim couldn't remember what room he was in. But

thankfully Joy had guessed that he might have trouble finding his way back to the room so she had conveniently left the motel door ajar. I gently pointed Slim through the door and then said goodnight to Noel and Keith.

Back in my own room I kicked off my shoes and was grateful for a soft bed to rest my weary bones on. It had been a long day. I was just about to doze off when the small motel was rocked by what I thought was an earth tremor. I went to sleep wondering if earth tremors on the Nullarbor were normal.

At breakfast the next morning I found out what had caused the earth tremor.

Keith Thompson had staggered into his motel room and done the best he could not to disturb his sleeping wife. He got undressed, kicked off his artificial leg (yes, Keith only has one leg) and endeavoured to hop to the toilet. He gained momentum, and the further he hopped the faster he went. Keith made it to the door of the toilet, tripped and fell head first into the gyprock wall behind the toilet. Keith's wife Carol thought he was dead but, apart from a hangover, Keith survived the night unscathed.

As a result of the boys' big night out in Eucla, Slim gave the Kenworth's sleeper cabin a thorough road test the next day.

Slim had been spending much of his time travelling with Thompson, who gave the legendary performer personal tuition on the gentle art of driving a road train. Slim was a quick learner and was soon behind the wheel of the big Kenworth. At the next truck stop he was beaming.

'It's the biggest vehicle I've ever driven. It's an amazing feeling up there. It's hard to

explain until you've done it and feel the power under your control.'

Keith's assessment of Slim's driving skills was positive: 'He took to it like a natural. He changed the gears so well. I reckon he's been outback somewhere near Longreach in one of those cattle road trains, practising. He wasn't tense at all.'

Slim's driving ability would be tested the next day when he asked for another bash at driving the road train. At the bottom of the Fraser Range, Slim was in the Kenworth's driver's seat for the windy, gear-jamming section of the narrowest bit of road between Adelaide and Perth. Once again he passed the test with flying colours.

'That's it for me,' Slim said. 'I've driven a road train and I don't need to do it again. I'm retiring undefeated.'

Keith and Noel had turned it on for Slim with their never-ending supply of truck stories, but on day four of the trip it was Slim's turn to return the favour. The place

was the side of the bitumen, halfway across the Nullarbor. The two Kenworths pulled over and Slim climbed down with his guitar in hand.

'"Lights on the Hill" was meant to be sung in front of a big Kenworth out here, so here we go:

*Windscreen wipers are beating in time,*
*The song they sing is a part of my mind ...'*

This was one impromptu concert that would never be forgotten by the crew and the two surprised tourists who just happened to be lucky enough to pass by. Two road trains in full flight also roared past mid-performance, their CB radios crackling instantly to life: 'I can't bloody turn around. Maybe I could drop the trailers and go back and see what's going on. I'm sure it was Slim Dusty.'

Almost everyone we ran into had their own Slim Dusty story. During the overnight break at the Balladonia Truck Stop, one

**ABOVE LEFT** Joy joined the road train hoping for inspiration writing new songs for Slim's *Making a Mile* album

**ABOVE** Slim catching up with Australian land speed record-holder Bill McGlashen member of a team of Nullarbor road workers recalled the days of the Roy Bell Boxing Troupe. Aged fifteen at the time, he had seen the Slim Dusty Show back in 1964. The pair traded yarns about life on the road.

'After being on the road for forty-three years I have come into contact with a lot of people, so it's natural that I run into many of them on my travels.'

This was Slim's simple explanation of this never-ending phenomenon.

The following day, it was lunch at the Norseman BP Truckstop. The Akubra-wearing manager Karen Harris already had Slim Dusty playing on the in-house music system when we arrived. Coincidentally, the staff had decided to have a country music

*Coincidentally, the staff had decided to have a country music day. They couldn't believe it when the man in the familiar hat walked in.*

day. They couldn't believe it when the man in the familiar hat walked in.

'No one told us Slim was coming,' Harris said. 'We got a big surprise, we didn't even know he was on the road.'

We drove on to Kalgoorlie and arrived at about 5 pm. We had been on the road for many long days and long nights. I was tired and looking forward to a good hot shower and a bit of a rest before we would all meet

for dinner. I had the shower and was just about to lie down when there was a knock on my door. It was Slim with guitar in hand.

'Joy wants to have a sleep and I feel like singing. Do you mind if I come in?' It would take a braver man than me to refuse Slim so in he came. He sat on the end of my bed while I made a cup of tea and listened. He knocked out song after song, picking and strumming his trusty Maton guitar. He was singing for the pure pleasure of it, because that is what he does. He doesn't need the excitement of a crowd or the charged atmosphere of the recording studio.

Watching and listening to Slim in my motel room, I realised he didn't even need me to listen. He was going to sing anyway. Singing is something that comes to Slim as naturally as breathing. It is something he has to do every day. I just happened to be lucky enough that day to be selected as the very exclusive audience for this one on one performance. He still takes great delight in singing his own songs. Some of the songs he has been singing for more than fifty years but in my motel room he was singing them with so much passion and heart you would swear he was singing them for the first time. There is never an ordinary performance from Slim.

A phone call interrupted this special performance but only long enough for me to say, 'Could you please call back later. I have Slim Dusty in my room singing requests.'

On to Perth to unhook the road train and deliver the semis to Thompsons Transport depot at Welshpool. Joy was serious when she climbed down from the Kenworth cab for the last time. 'I'm just getting warmed up, I could keep going forever.'

The final dinner together for the crew in Perth was a time to swap memories and yarns and even make plans for future trips. Slim had been particularly impressed by the friendly folk at Eucla, so Thompson, Brown and Slim were already looking at putting on a show to end all shows right in the middle of the Nullarbor.

'It would be a good opportunity to get all the truck drivers, the country music people and the locals together,' said Brown.

Thompson chipped in, 'We can use one of my tautliners for a stage and we can truck in toilets and generators'.

'Let's do it,' Slim said. 'I'll get some of my mates in country music over to perform.'

Look out Eucla!

Everyone voted the trip a huge success. Said Joy, 'I have enough raw material to keep writing songs for years. I have three definite song ideas that I hope will make Slim's truck album.'

'Just write another "Lights on the Hill",' was Slim's constant challenge to his wife during the trip.

The trip had served its purpose. Joy McKean did write three songs for the album, and Slim was mentally prepared to hit the studio, feeling more than comfortable about recording an authentic Aussie truck album.

*Makin' a Mile*, Slim Dusty's ninety-third album, is the result of that epic truck trip across the Nullarbor.

**ABOVE** Slim taking a breather after his impromtu concert beside the road trains in the middle of the Nullarbor

# Slim's Solomon Islands Celebration

## 1998

The people of the Solomon Islands love to sing and dance, and Slim Dusty's third visit to this tropical paradise had the locals screaming for more. Slim had made the trip twice before, once in 1969 with his guitar player Barry Thornton, and again in 1986 with The Travelling Country Band for a concert after Cyclone Namu had hit the islands.

**LEFT**  Slim's concert in the Solomon Islands attracted more people than the Queen's official visit

The Solomons are a pretty exotic place, being part of the Oceania group in the South Pacific and about a four-hour flight north-east of Australia. Slim's prior visits had made a big impact and it was obvious that many of the older residents had fond memories of him and held him in high esteem. His visits had also influenced some of the local singer–songwriters, including Fred Maedora and Tom Stranger, the latter even having written his own songs in the Slim Dusty style.

The reason for Slim's visit this time was to perform at a series of goodwill concerts during the week-long activities for the opening of the Gold Ridge Mine.

*A couple of youngsters told me they liked the music but most of all they liked the stories that 'Mr Slim' told.*

'I didn't need a lot of convincing when asked to come to the Solomons,' Slim said. 'It seems like my second home. I really love the country and the people.'

Slim's Solomon schedule was a busy one with a concert for VIPs, a performance for the landowners at the Lungga resettlement village, an impromptu performance for hospital patients in Honiara, the capital, and the grand finale concert before a capacity crowd of twenty thousand cheering fans at Lawson Tama, the main football field in Honiara.

This concert was one of the biggest ever seen in the Solomons, with a massive sound system flown in from Australia for the event. The sound equipment completely filled a large jet freighter and the mining company

built a special stage at the venue in the shape of a traditional Solomon Islands hut.

I watched some of the concert with one of the members of the Islands' parliament, and he said to me, 'There are more people here to see Slim than there were to see the Queen, but then again, the Queen didn't sing'.

Many in the crowd were obviously too young to have any memories of Slim's previous visits but this didn't stop them enjoying the music.

A couple of youngsters told me they liked the music but most of all they liked the stories that 'Mr Slim' told.

**ABOVE** Part of the large crowd which came to the concert at the Lungga resettlement village

**RIGHT** Many people who came to see Slim remembered him from his earlier visits to the island in 1969 and 1986

**BELOW** A cultural exchange: Slim with some of the local performers dressed in their tribal costume

**LEFT** The children loved fiddle player Peter Denahy and mimicked his fiddle playing for days afterwards

One of the big hits that night was band member Peter Denahy's fiddle playing. Apparently the fiddle is fairly rare in this part of the Pacific so every time Peter stepped forward to play a solo on his instrument the crowd went wild. Walking through Honiara for the next couple of days I was amazed to see many young children imitating Peter's playing on improvised fiddles.

During my stay in the Solomons I also shot a twenty-minute video of Slim's visit for Ross Mining and was lucky enough to stay on after the concert to edit the video at a state-of-the-art digital video editing facility in the heart of Honiara.

We worked twelve hours a day editing that video, the consolation being that the edit suite featured a huge picture window overlooking the Honiara waterfront. The view of this tropical paradise tortured me all week. However, some of the locals I worked with drove me to the beach at the end of the week for my only Pacific Ocean dip.

Bertus De Graff, CEO of Ross Mining, who arranged for Slim to visit said, 'Slim is a real legend and the people of the Solomon Islands have a genuine love for him. They love his music and his honesty.'

**BELOW** Slim with Solomon Island entertainer Fred Maedora, who compered some of the shows

# Slim's Guitar Players

Tex Morton, Buddy Williams and Slim Dusty all did their bit to pioneer the real sound of Australia, the Australian bush ballad. One of them, Slim, took the bush ballad and made it his own. Sixty years and one hundred and three albums down the track, the man is still making great music — music that is real, passionate and relevant and, most importantly, Australian.

**LEFT** Slim and his much-loved Maton guitar with Travelling Country Band member Jeff Mercer and his battered Fender

There are many components to the Slim Dusty sound; the lyrics are real, the voice is as Australian as the wide open spaces of the Aussie outback … and there is that unique Slim Dusty guitar sound.

Over Slim's career, there have been a number of guitar players who have contributed to that Slim Dusty guitar sound. Many of them have done their bit in the studio but only a select few have become members of the elite who have played with Slim in the studio *and* on the road. Slim and six of his most important guitar players tell us about their part in the Slim Dusty guitar sound:

**ABOVE** Slim's custom-built Maton guitar

### SLIM DUSTY

'I taught myself to play guitar off 78 records and when I sounded like the record I figured I was on the right track.

'I use a thumb pick, which is pretty unusual today – it gives you a very solid foundation for rhythm and is the style used by some of the old cowboy singers like Gene Autry, Jimmie Rodgers and Tex Morton. It is called the pick 'n' strum style and is perfect for story songs and ballads.

'When I hit the showgrounds in the '50s, I was working with just my guitar but pretty soon I had Joy on bass and Barry Thornton, who was developing his lead guitar style, on guitar. We called ourselves The Bushlanders. That was when we really concreted the bush-ballad guitar sound. The Bushlanders were my band for years but in the early '70s Barry left and over a period of time we developed

the Travelling Country Band which is still with me today.

'I record with a big Bicentennial Commemorative Limited Edition D–76 Martin. These days I'm using Maton guitars on stage and they are working very well and I am happy to use Maton because we have both been going a bit over fifty years.'

### BARRY THORNTON

Barry played with Slim from 1954 till 1974.

'I joined Slim for three months as a singer and comedian on his touring show and those three months lasted twenty years. Eventually my singing went out the window and my guitar playing came to the fore.

'I started out with an old Swedish guitar, a Levin. But it got busted on one of our trips so I bought a Gibson for nine hundred and something pounds that I didn't have. That Gibson was the basis of Slim's electric guitar sound. It is a Gibson ES 335 Round Dot Original. I bought it in 1963 but I think the guitar was actually made in 1959. It still has the original Humbucker pickups in it; it even has the original volume and tone controls. Everything is absolutely original. The machine heads, the tuning pegs, all original.

*I am happy to use Maton because we have both been going a bit over fifty years.*

'My first real amp was a Moody, and they were a good old amp too. We then had a Fender Bandmaster with forty or sixty watts. My Gibson with the Bandmaster was the original Slim Dusty guitar sound.

'I will not use effects pedals because I believe you should be able to produce on stage what you produce in the studio. I just don't use them.

'Some of my favourite Slim Dusty songs that I played on include "Winterwinds" which has become a standard, "By a Fire of Gidgee Coal" and "Born to be a Rolling Stone". Slim has a distinctive guitar playing style, not so much the sound but the style. When you get a good pick 'n' strum player like Slim it is about the best rhythm you can get. It is an absolute country sound.'

**ABOVE**  Slim and Jeff Mercer tuning up backstage at the Longreach Civic Centre

## LINDSAY BUTLER

Lindsay has been playing with Slim on and off since 1972.

'I moved to Tamworth in 1972 to try to get more involved with the country music business and before I knew it I had a job playing guitar for Slim. Our first concert was at Bourke and after that first night everyone was looking for old Baz, as this was the first time Slim had toured without Barry Thornton.

'I played a 1968 Fender Jazzmaster and it is a pretty rare one because it was made when CBS owned the company and not Leo Fender. Everything is stock standard, the pickups were designed for this guitar and have never been changed. I've had the guitar for thirty years and I think the guitar has stood up better than I have. It has only been re-fretted once and painted once or twice.

'I used a Musicman amp when I was with Slim and also a Fender amp in the studio a couple of times. Some of my favourite songs I recorded with Slim include "Things I See Around Me", "Old Gilbert", "Catching Yellowbelly" and "Three Rivers Hotel".'

## CHARLEY BOYTER

Charley recorded with Slim in 1975 and his first tour was 1976. He has worked with Slim on and off ever since.

'I got the first call to record with Slim in 1975. Initially I played a bit of rhythm. In 1976 Slim phoned and asked if I'd like to do a tour to the west. I said yes and had to go and get my first electric guitar, an L Series Telecaster. When Slim said we were going west I thought he meant Orange, Bathurst and Dubbo. Our first show was Coolgardie. It was west all right. Before the tour I had a crash course in electric guitar from Lindsay Butler. That tour was the first professional gig I ever did.

'I have played on a lot of Slim's recording sessions and was on his fortieth, fiftieth, sixtieth, seventieth, eightieth and ninetieth albums. I wasn't on every track but had

> *I think the guitar has stood up better than I have. It has only been re-fretted once and painted once or twice.*

material on all those albums. My lead picking and his rhythm picking work well together. I still enjoy getting together and playing with Slim.

'Mainly I used an acoustic 1967 Martin D-18 guitar. When I joined Slim I started to play most of the lead on acoustic, not on electric as Barry and Lindsay had in the past. Most of Slim's recorded material from 1975 to 1990 had my acoustic lead. Most of the time I played through a Fender twin amp. Probably the song I liked best was "A Letter from Arrabury", which is unusual because I actually played electric lead on it. It was also probably the most difficult song I recorded with Slim. The other song that sticks in my memory is "Leave Him in the Long Yard", from around 1977.'

### IAN SIMPSON

Ian was a member of Slim's band for a period in the early '80s and again in the '90s. He played with Slim for a total of twelve years.

'I was a 21-year-old banjo player when Slim asked if I would like to join his band. Obviously I said yes and was with Slim as banjo and dobro player and a little bit of rhythm for a year and a half. I came back in to the band in 1990 as lead player. Over the years I think I ended up playing lead on about twelve or thirteen albums.

'Slim soon let me know he wanted me to play his old songs my way.

'One of the things about all of Slim's guitar players, they all played close to the bridge and that gives you that really hard sound. That was Barry's thing. It's great when you do the old bush ballads, to go into that sound and use a certain guitar setting. If you combine the two pickups you get a real clunky Barry Thornton sound. That is the sound to have in your mind when you do the old songs.

'When you are playing on stage with Slim it is important to hear his voice and his guitar. If you are not sure of where the beat is

*Slim has the best rhythm of anyone I have ever played with.*

going you just look at his leg. If Slim moves his leg a certain way he means to slow down. You wouldn't call Slim a flash guitarist but he is as strong as anything. His rhythm playing really astounds me. Slim has the best rhythm of anyone I have ever played with.

'When I played with The Flying Emus we were touring through Victoria and Ian Noyes, the great guitar maker, came up and offered to make me a guitar. After chatting with Ian he said that he already had made a guitar that fitted what I wanted. It had two really nice and expensive EMG pickups. There was only one problem, the guitar was pink! Eventually I added a third pickup which gives me some Stratocaster sounds as well and I changed the colour to baby blue. This is the guitar I used all through my Slim days.

## COLIN WATSON

Colin played guitar with Slim in '74 and '75.

'I just happened to be around when Slim was looking for a guitar player – it fell into my lap by accident. My choice was to join Slim's band or join the public service. I think I made the right choice.

'I didn't have a clue who Slim was or know that much about his music. I did like the country rock thing that was happening in the early '70s so I was familiar with the music in general and I simply shaped my style to suit Slim. "Biggest Disappointment"

and "Indian Pacific" were two of the first songs I played on in the studio. When it came time to do "Indian Pacific", which was a bit of a change for Slim, he knew exactly what he wanted. I just had to come up with the appropriate arrangement. It surprised me a bit because we really rocked on that one.

'Slim dictates the pace, and he is definitely the boss. He has good musical tastes, knows what he wants and when to do it, when to make changes.

'During my time with Slim I was playing a late 1950s semi-acoustic Epiphone Coronado. I was into Wes Montgomery at the time and

**ABOVE** Four of Slim's guitar players all on stage at the one time at the 'Hats Off to Slim' concert at the Tamworth regional Entertainment Centre in 2000. From left, Charley Boyter, Barry Thornton, Lindsay Butler and Ian Simpson that is what he was playing. I really wanted a Dwayne Eddy Gretsch but couldn't afford one. The Epiphone is the one that produced the memorable intro on "Indian Pacific". I was using a Fender, affectionately known as "Fred the Fender". It was all original with Jensen speakers. It was Slim's amp and he still has it. I didn't use pedals or effects.'

In 1997 Colin got to co-produce Slim's jazz-inspired album *A Time to Remember* with Rod Coe. 'Slim sings as good as Tony Bennett on this one,' Colin said. 'Slim is an absolutely beautiful human being.'

## JEFF MERCER

Jeff has been Slim's guitar player for the past five years.

'I had never seen Slim play live. I went along to the audition with no preconceived notion of what I was to do; I just turned up and played and got the job. I was impressed when Slim actually phoned and told me I had the job.

'We went straight into the studio and started recording the *Country Way of Life* CD. You can imagine trying to get a handle on Slim's back catalogue. After ninety-five albums there are so many facets to all the different styles of guitar playing. There are really traditional bush ballads from the early days right through to contemporary-sounding bush ballads such as "Ringer from the Top End", which rock up the sound a bit. For a while the live shows were more and more like a rock and roll production.

'I play a very old and very battered Fender Telecaster and used a Musicman amp that is equally as battered. I've had the same gear for the past seventeen years. About every five years or so the old Telecaster comes apart and everything gets replaced. It gets a re-fret, new tuners, new nuts, new bridge, new everything. Almost like a fifteen thousand kilometre check-up for a car. It has Texas Special Custom Shop Telecaster pickups.

'I have only started using effects in recent years after playing straight through my amp for years and years. I would vary the tone through my pickup selector, playing back by the bridge or a little closer, changing pickup selection in the middle of a song.

'In the studio we go for live takes. We go for a good take on Slim's vocal which is totally arse-about to how most people do it. We go for Slim's vocal every time. If I screw up it doesn't matter because we can go back

**RIGHT** One-time member of The Happening Thang and now Slim's guitar player, Jeff Mercer

and fix my bit later. If we get it in the first take, that's the one we use.

'*Makin' a Mile*, the last trucking album, was a magnificent studio experience. We were just going take after take. '91 over 50' was good in the studio as well. It was just happening, takes were going down and we were really flying through the songs. Sometimes on stage I use a baritone guitar which was built by Piers Crocker.'

## ROD COE

Rod Coe joined Slim as record producer in 1976 and later took over the role of bass player in Slim's touring band.

'At the time I was house producer at EMI. I hit it off with Slim instantly and have been working with him ever since.

'When Slim is looking for a new guitar player, he looks for someone who will create their own version of Slim's style. Slim hasn't changed the essence of his music over the years but he is always willing to try new things and new players. I think he enjoys seeing how far he can go, without ever getting away from the core of what Slim Dusty is.

'He hasn't changed drastically on the music front but he certainly has evolved. He has a more relaxed approach to what he does today. In the studio and on stage I know instinctively what Slim is doing. It is very much a feel thing with Slim.

I use a 1964 Fender Precision bass guitar which has a jazz pickup added and a D tuner. I play it through a Nemesis bass amp.'

## OTHER GUITAR PLAYERS WHO HAVE PLAYED WITH SLIM IN THE STUDIO:

| | |
|---|---|
| Don Andrews | Kelvin Nolan |
| Phil Emmanuel | Mark Punch |
| Tommy Emmanuel | Mick Reid |
| Stewart French | Alan Rhodes |
| George Golla | Keith Urban |
| Lawrie Minson | Graham Wardrop |

**ABOVE** Rod Coe has been Slim's producer, bass player and band leader of the Travelling Country Band for many years

# Back on the Farm

In recognition of Slim's incredible contribution to music in Australia, and as a tribute to the special place he holds in the hearts of all Australians, Kempsey Shire Council is in the process of establishing the Slim Dusty Heritage Centre, a museum dedicated to the life of Slim Dusty.

**LEFT** Slim on the bank of Nulla Nulla Creek near his childhood home illed with memorabilia donated by Slim and Joy, the Slim Dusty Heritage Centre will feature interactive displays, travelling exhibitions, educational facilities, a theatre for live entertainment and a recording studio.

Importantly, it is Slim and Joy's wish that the centre's profits be given back to the community in the form of scholarships for young musicians.

Other country music pioneers from the Kempsey area will be featured in the centre. 'So much country music came from the north coast,' Joy explained. 'It all needs to be remembered, as well as Slim.' Slim and Joy's recent purchase of his childhood home means that visitors to the proposed Heritage Centre in the main part of Kempsey will also be able to make the journey to Nulla Nulla Creek to see where Slim grew up.

As a child, Slim called the farm Melody Ranch, but the Dusty's have renamed it Homeward Farm. When they drove around their 'new' farm, they were amazed by its beauty.

'It is some of the most beautiful country, with timber going right to the top of the ridge and past that is all National Park,' says Joy.

**BELOW** There's no slowing down for Slim and Joy, seen here discussing plans for Homeward Farm

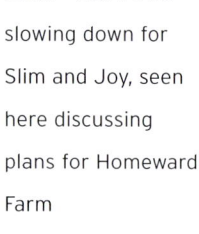

**LEFT** Slim's family home, Homeward Farm at Nulla Nulla, will eventually be refurbished and open to the public

**LEFT** This is the road Slim walked as a teenager when he left the family farm in the late '40s to pursue a career that would far surpass his wildest dreams

# Tales from the Road

Over the past ten years I have been lucky enough to travel with Slim Dusty on his many tours and adventures. Slim loves the open road and he is quite happy to sit back and enjoy the view of the Australian landscape rushing past the windscreen. He is a born showman and can keep his travelling mates entertained for hours with stories from his early days.

**LEFT** Slim and his much-travelled red teapot

**PREVIOUS PAGE** Joy McKean and Slim with daughter Anne in the early '50s

Slim could easily write a book on the motels of Australia. Often while travelling he will be mid-sentence and a small motel will flash past and without pausing for a breath he will give a quick opinion on the motel. 'Nice people run that place', 'Bloody old towels in that place', or 'We stayed there back in 1974'.

Even though Slim sings most nights of the week it's not unusual for him to also sing ditties for hours on the road. Once he kept me amused all the way from Renmark to Adelaide. From the looks on the faces of Joy and daughter Anne that day it was obvious that they had heard some of Slim's silly songs before but I loved it and howled with laughter.

Slim's yarns from the road cover a lot of territory:

'Joy and I hit the road in 1954 and headed north in the old '38 Ford. Our daughter Anne was with us and she was only about two. The boys, Barry Thornton and Malcolm Mason, made up the rest of our troupe and they had a tent to sleep in behind the halls.

*I never thought that fifty years later we'd still be doing it. I suppose I didn't look that far ahead.*

'Our very small show left Sydney for a three-month trial run and went up the coast, just into Queensland and came back down the New England highway and played every whistle stop. We never made a lot of money, but we could see there were possibilities there.

'The following year we went out for twelve months and took Johnny Ashcroft and his wife with us and went down into Victoria. Victoria was not very friendly to travelling shows in those days and we froze down there. It's quite strange, but Victoria could now just about be one of our best states.

'Next trip we went way up to North Queensland, again with Johnny Ashcroft. We went into Queensland and headed west out through Roma, Charleville, up through all the towns to Longreach, out to Muttaburra, and across country to Hughenden and Richmond. We came through Charters Towers over the coast at Townsville, struck rain and black soil plains all the way through the west. I never thought that fifty years later we'd still be doing it. I suppose I didn't look that far ahead.

'Show life and entertainment gets in your blood. I identify with the outlook of circus people and the show-ground people. Once you become a showman you are always a showman and have a showman's outlook. The showies look after each other. The word spreads: "don't go to that town, it's a graveyard, just stay away from there".

'It was a way of life. No one can understand unless they have done it. On the road, nine or ten months with four or five caravans and living as a travelling family. That was the real show life. We would have Sunday night off, and we'd go bush if the country permitted it. We would pull up about two o'clock or three o'clock in the afternoon, and find a secluded spot, way off

the highway, draw the vans into a circle and then we'd have an hour wood gathering. We'd have a big barbecue. It was a good life. It's not the same today.

'You had to have a good team with you and in the early days we had a chap called Teddy Trevor, from the show grounds. He was a cousin of Frank Foster who was the promoter of the big shows we had on the show grounds – part of the Foster family.

'Teddy came with us and he was a great advance man. In lots of cases, the bookings were left to him. He knew what distances we could safely travel, so sometimes he had to put us into small places.

'We had to be into a town no later than about two or three o'clock in the afternoon. This gave us time to park the caravans, then the boys would have a meal, and would go and set up. Not an elaborate set up mind

*You could only travel short distances and you had to look after your vehicles. It was a pretty set routine.*

you, but the curtains had to go up, seats had to be looked at, and things like that. The dozing hour was about four or five o'clock. We would have a doze in the afternoon because showing six or seven nights a week, you needed one.

'We had to travel slow because of the roads. You could only travel short distances and you had to look after your vehicles. It was a pretty set routine. We were rolling by nine. With the truck, you'd have to check

tyres and check the diesel every day before you hit the road. On the big trips around Australia we carried forty-four gallon drums of diesel.

'Going around the same places every year we got know all the blokes in the service stations and the people in the shops. Joy knew the dress shops and places where she could buy some decent things. Charleville was a friendly town and it still is.

'We went into a shop in Tennant Creek once and this bloke says, "I went to your show last night, and bought a bag of peanuts. You want to watch the bloke that's looking after your peanuts".

'I said, "What's wrong with them?" He said, "Mate, they had a taste of diesel or petrol".

'One of the drums of fuel must have leaked a bit. We had old Mack Cormack with us and he was the peanut man. Some of the peanuts were a little bit tainted ...

'The mining towns like Kalgoorlie always made us welcome. In those days we never stayed more than two days anywhere but we used to play Kalgoorlie for a week.

'Mount Isa was good to us as well. We eventually got it all worked out when we were planning our tours. We'd always be in Mount Isa rodeo week. There were always big crowds with lots of stockmen coming in from everywhere.

'The first time we ever did the big trip out west was in the early '60s and we headed for Darwin. We'd never been past Mount Isa before. We were with Frank Foster then and were the first big tent show to go into the Northern Territory. We had Samson the Strongman and other people with us.

'We had to charge ten shillings admittance to cover expenses and to work our way back. We showed at the Darwin show and came back to Mount Isa. We thought maybe we'd get a couple of nights in the Isa but we showed for about a week and a half. When it came time to leave Mount Isa, people came with green vegetables from their garden just to help us along the track. They were good times.

'We have a lot of country to cover in Australia and we have some pretty good roads in comparison to the size of our country. In the early days some of the roads were a little rough.

*We had old Mack Cormack with us and he was the peanut man. Some of the peanuts were a little bit tainted ...*

'Today we have the same amount of sound equipment as a rock and roll show. We have to have the good sound and lighting effects now. There's one truck that carries the gear and the road crew of three or four blokes. We hire four or five cars. If the trips are too long for Joy and me, we fly.

'The change in our touring was a gradual thing just like our music has changed. My first ever version of "Lights on the Hill" is still recognisable but is very different from how I do it today. Change happens.

**LEFT** At about 9 o'clock every morning the cars are loaded up for the drive to the next town

RIGHT  Slim and his
promoter Arthur
Laing share a joke

RIGHT  Still going
strong after fifty
years of touring

'The show's much bigger now, much larger. The expenses are sky high so we have to go to the big places. The outback people in many cases are more hip than some of the city people. They're pretty smart.

'It was okay in the early days because we were all a lot younger. I've got a bit more used to comfort now. I'm still in the game, and I'll always stay in the game. I'll always want to travel, keep touring and I'll always want to keep recording as long as I can.

'My first trip into the bush was an eye-opener for me ... We went out around Bathurst and further west into New South Wales. That was my first experience of how the flat country just went on and on and on.

'Eventually, when we started travelling ourselves, we went to western Queensland and then across the Nullarbor. We got very used to the outback. The outback grows on you, it definitely grows on you. Distances are so vast and it's so open. When we came back to the coast we felt hemmed in.

'The bush isn't a lonely thing, it's very friendly really. I did a song years ago that summed it up well: "It's a hard, hard country and to be out there you've got to be a hard hard man."

'That's about it!'

*The outback people are far more advanced and in many cases more hip than some of the city people.*

**RIGHT** Slim Dusty and the Travelling Country Band. From left, Mike Kerrin on fiddle, Rod Coe on bass, Rob Souter on drums, Slim, Jeff Mercer on guitar and part-time band member Peter Denahy on accordian

**RIGHT** Slim and Joy climbing the steps of Sydney's Town Hall

**RIGHT** Slim and Joy on the road between Charters Towers and Ravenswood in north Queensland

**LEFT** Slim and Richard Tognetti from the Australian Chamber Orchestra at the Sydney Town Hall

**LEFT** With a statue of the swaggie from 'Waltzing Matilda' in Winton

**FOLLOWING PAGE** 'I've walked a mile or two in my lifetime': Slim in the Kimberley scrub

# The Cover Story

'Getting my picture taken is part of the job,' Slim admits. 'John and I have done about ten covers together now. We know when we're in a good spot and when it's going to work. If it's not going to work, we simply move to another spot.'

**LEFT** On an abandoned rail track at Silverton near Broken Hill

'We've done all kinds of shots. I've been freezing, I've been hot, I've been standing in water and almost getting blown off a hill.'

Slim actively gets involved in the planning of all of his album covers. During the recording sessions he will often phone to bounce a cover idea off me. Slim always has definite ideas on what he wants on the cover of his new CD but his ideas can change, especially if we shoot the cover image while he is touring.

I like all the covers, but not all for the same reasons.

*Ringer from the Top End* marked a change in Slim's cover photography. I thought that Slim was well-enough known that his head and shoulders didn't have to fill the cover of the CD. This shot almost has a *National Geographic* feel to it. Slim is working with the men in the yards at Carlton Hill Station. The early morning light, the dust, the bush and Slim in the middle of it all makes for a memorable image.

*Makin' a Mile* is also one of my favourites. There is something about the sight of a big road train on the Nullarbor. The colour of the trucks against the blue sky, with Slim looking pretty comfortable in front of them, produced an iconic image.

Slim has been photographed so many times he has a set of 'looks' that he uses in front of the camera. I guess it is his way of guaranteeing the photographer gets a good shot every time. The image on the cover of '99 is the most natural shot I ever took of Slim and for that reason it is my favourite. We did the shot in his backyard when he had proudly shown me his chooks. Maybe that is why he looks so happy.

There was a lot of pressure to come up with a killer image for Slim's 100th album, *Looking Forward, Looking Back*. We talked about it for months and had a lot of input from Leon Concannon from the record company. Somehow we came up with the idea to photograph Slim in the Simpson Desert. I was on tour in Victoria with Slim but once again we were running out of time. I mentioned our desert idea to a couple of the locals in Mildura and they told me about the sand hills at Wentworth, about thirty minutes away.

The next morning, John Arnold, a mate of mine who runs the Mildura Festival, picked Slim and me up before sunrise and off we headed. We drove through the vineyards, across the Murray River, through historic Wentworth and out of town into the open country. Just as the sun was rising we spotted them, right in the middle of a paddock of waving grass, the most beautiful red sand hills you could ever imagine. They were just like the sand hills I hoped we would find in the Simpson Desert.

Even before I had shot one frame, I knew that we would get an image worthy of the

*The early morning light, the dust, the bush and Slim in the middle of it all makes for a memorable image.*

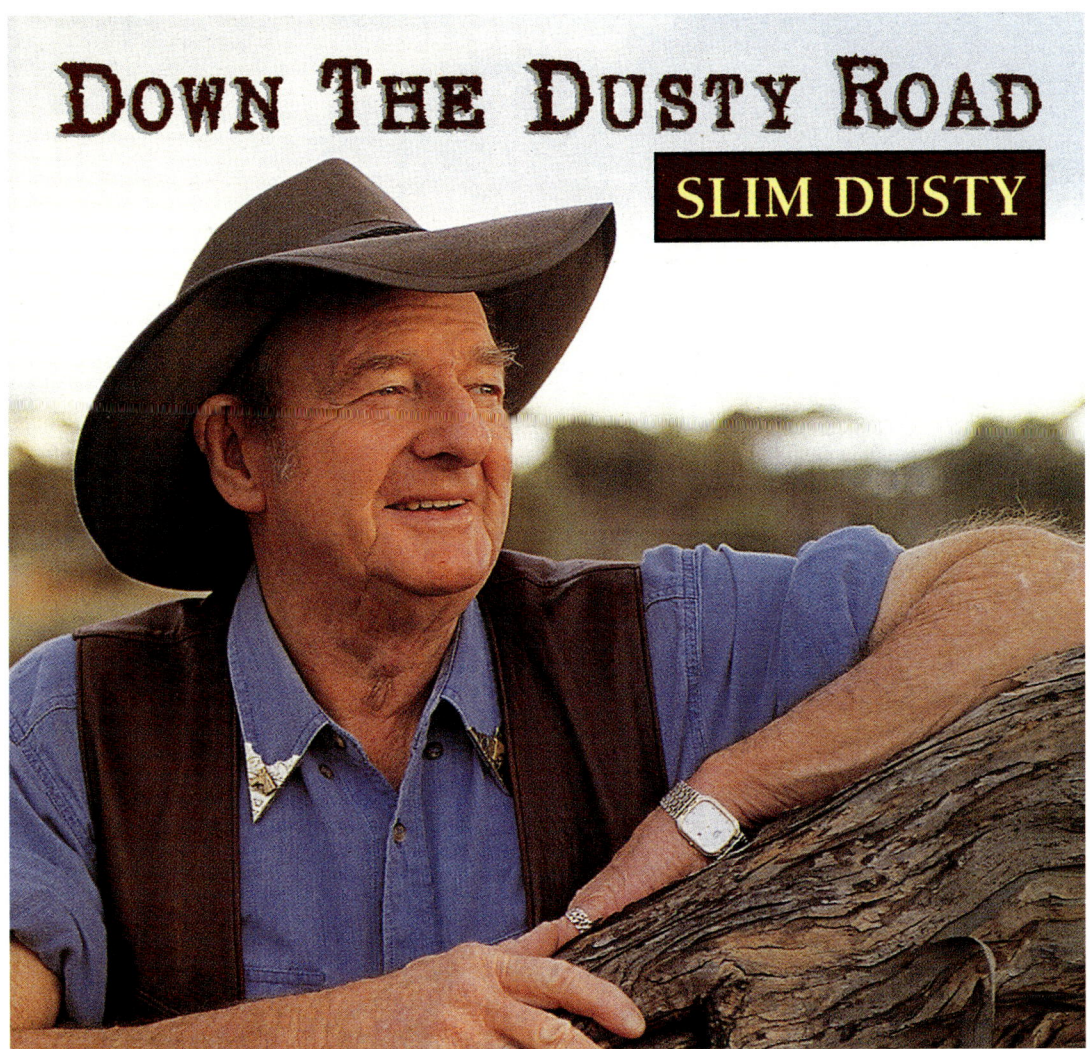

100th cover. I phoned Leon and he asked if I would snap a couple of shots of windmills, old shed and old trees. Leon had an idea.

Back in Sydney I got my film processed and dropped it into the record company. Leon liked the photos and called in Mark Jago who is Slim's video producer and also an expert in the digital manipulation of images.

Mark coupled the tree, shed and windmill with the shot of Slim in the desert and we had the cover image. Mark also produced one of the best music videos ever when he made the video clip for 'Looking Forward, Looking Back'.

You might be interested to hear what Slim himself thinks of the CD covers …

## DOWN THE DUSTY ROAD

'This is a reissue. The new shot was taken by John at the back of one of the motels we stayed at on the Nullarbor when we did the trip on the road trains to shoot the cover for *Makin' a Mile*.'

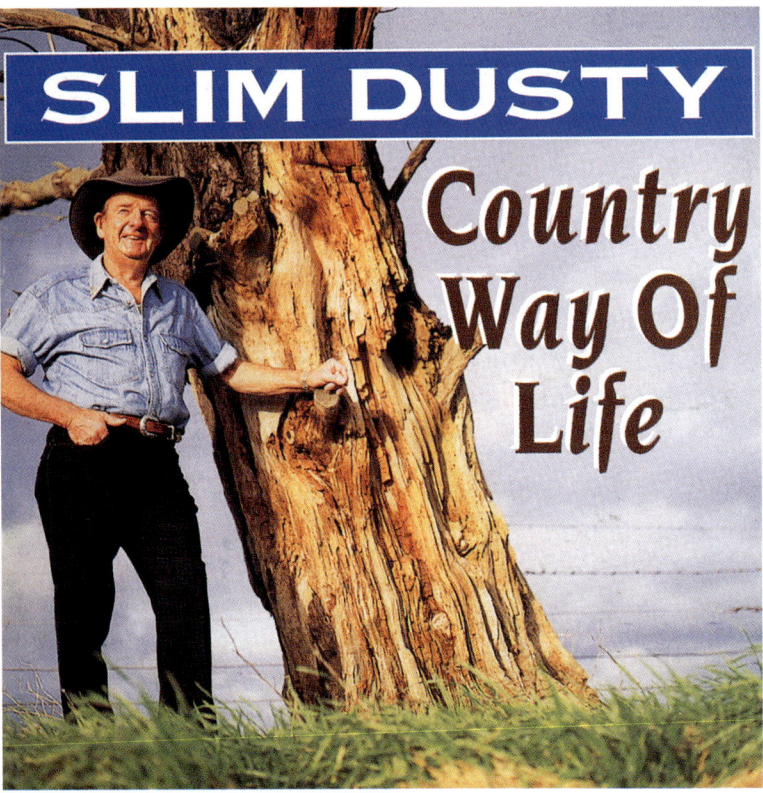

### SLIM DUSTY SINGS JOY McKEAN

'We shot that on a cold afternoon outside Ballarat ... I remember it was a very, very cold afternoon. There was a beautiful green pasture behind us. Joy and I look extremely happy which is strange because it was bloody cold.'

### RINGER FROM THE TOP END

'That's an outstanding picture because it's so typical of that part of Australia. It was about six o'clock in the morning, working with the men up at Carlton Hill in the Kimberley.'

### NATURAL HIGH

'This was shot at Gowrie Station near Charleville. The country looked beautiful at the time. The Mobbs family owns the station and this is where Alistair Jones wrote the "Flying Doctors Ball". We stayed there and had a great time with the Mobbs family. We had the use of their kitchen and enjoyed using the old stove. I need to go back to this country at least once a year to enrich myself. There's definitely a spirit that comes from being in the bush.'

### COUNTRY WAY OF LIFE

'When John took this picture I was standing up to my ankles in cold muddy water, but I still had to smile. We had been on the road for days and it rained every day. John and I headed off early one morning, just north of Warrnambool, and there was a break in the clouds for about ten minutes and we got the shot.'

SLIM DUSTY
RINGER FROM THE TOP END

Natural High
· SLIM DUSTY ·

SLIM DUSTY
MAKIN' A MILE
BE AWARE! THIS ALBUM GOES WHERE NO 'STAR TRUCKER' HAS GONE BEFORE.

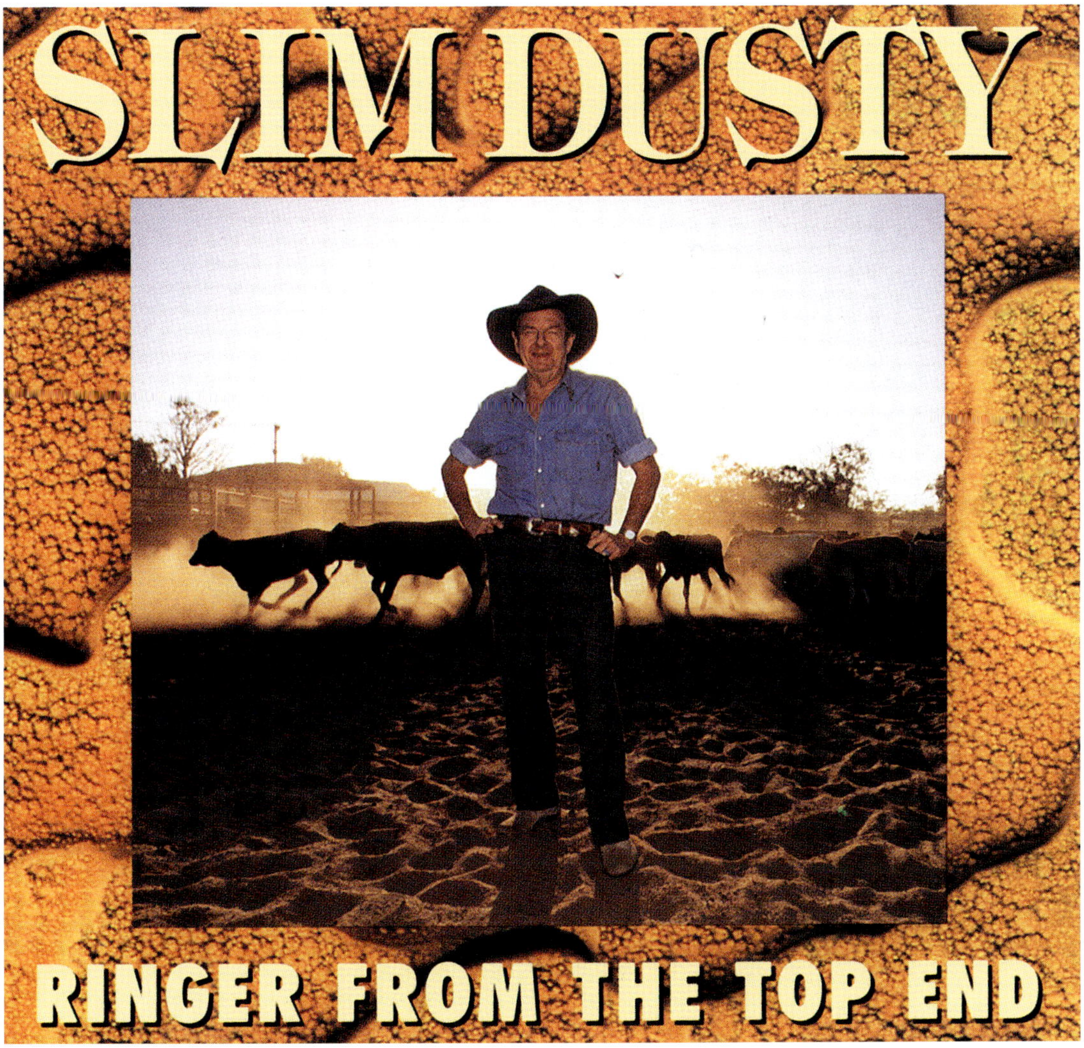

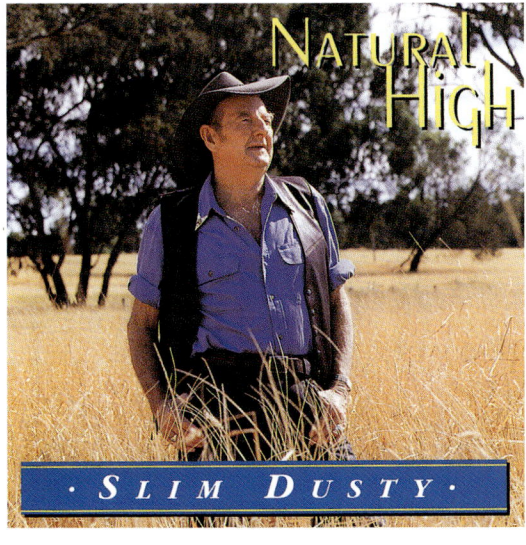

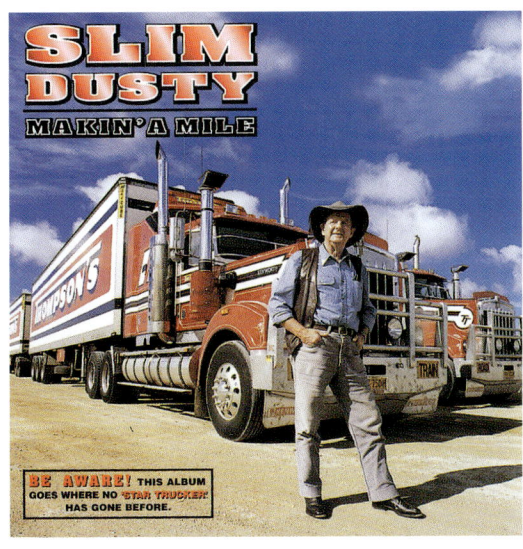

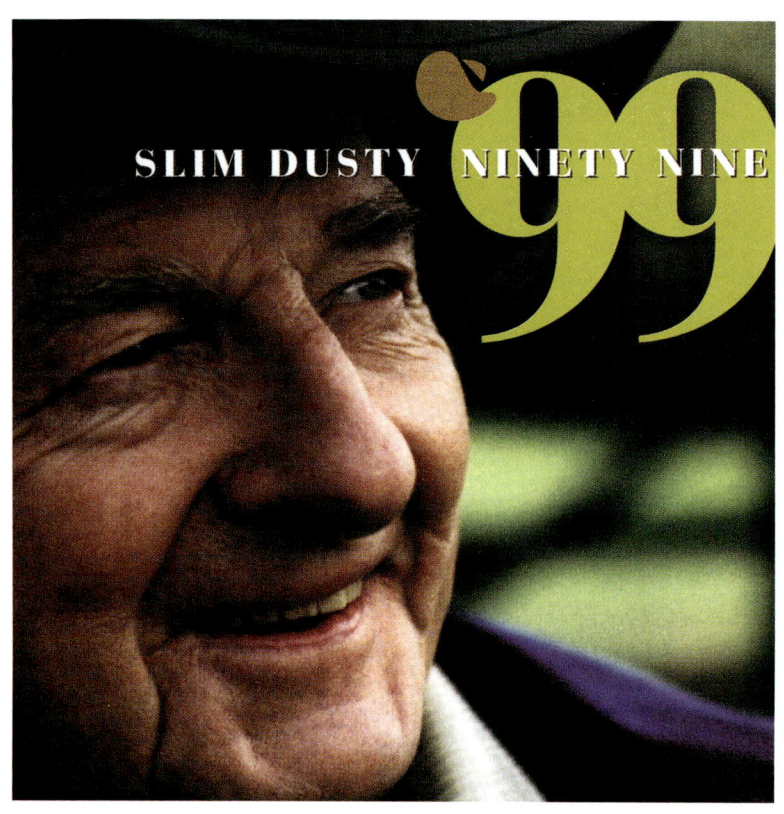

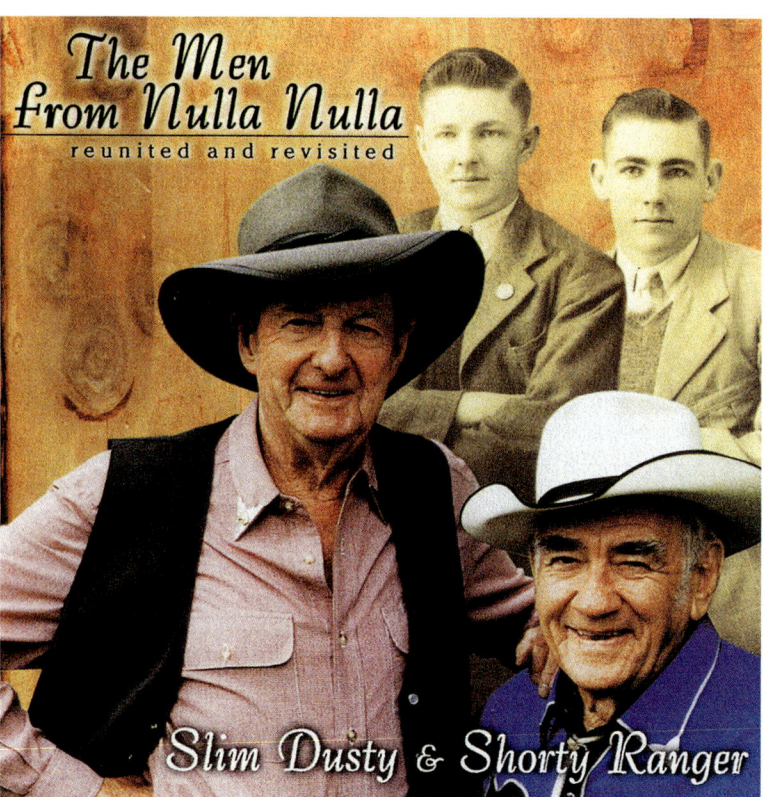

### MAKIN' A MILE

'An easy shot to do. The big open spaces of the Nullarbor and the big road trains. I liked the colour of the trucks against the blue sky.'

### '99

"'99 was recorded in my office at home. I put down a lot of talking stories and monologues and I had great satisfaction doing that. I had a little sign outside the office door, "Keep Out" and I think that's still there. John took these photos in my back yard, probably the easiest cover we ever shot.'

### LOOKING FORWARD, LOOKING BACK

'Out from Wentworth, near Mildura ... acres and acres of sand. It could be in the middle of the desert, the way it photographed. But, yeah, it sort of suited the album very well. The stance was right, and the shirt and the trousers all came up. And they decorated it of course with a little hut and a few things.'

### THE MEN FROM NULLA NULLA – REUNITED AND REVISITED

'It was great to record with my childhood friend Shorty Ranger. We had been mates for sixty years and finally Shorty came down to Sydney and recorded with me. It was an amazing day and it went so smooth. We did the photos on the day Shorty recorded his vocals.'

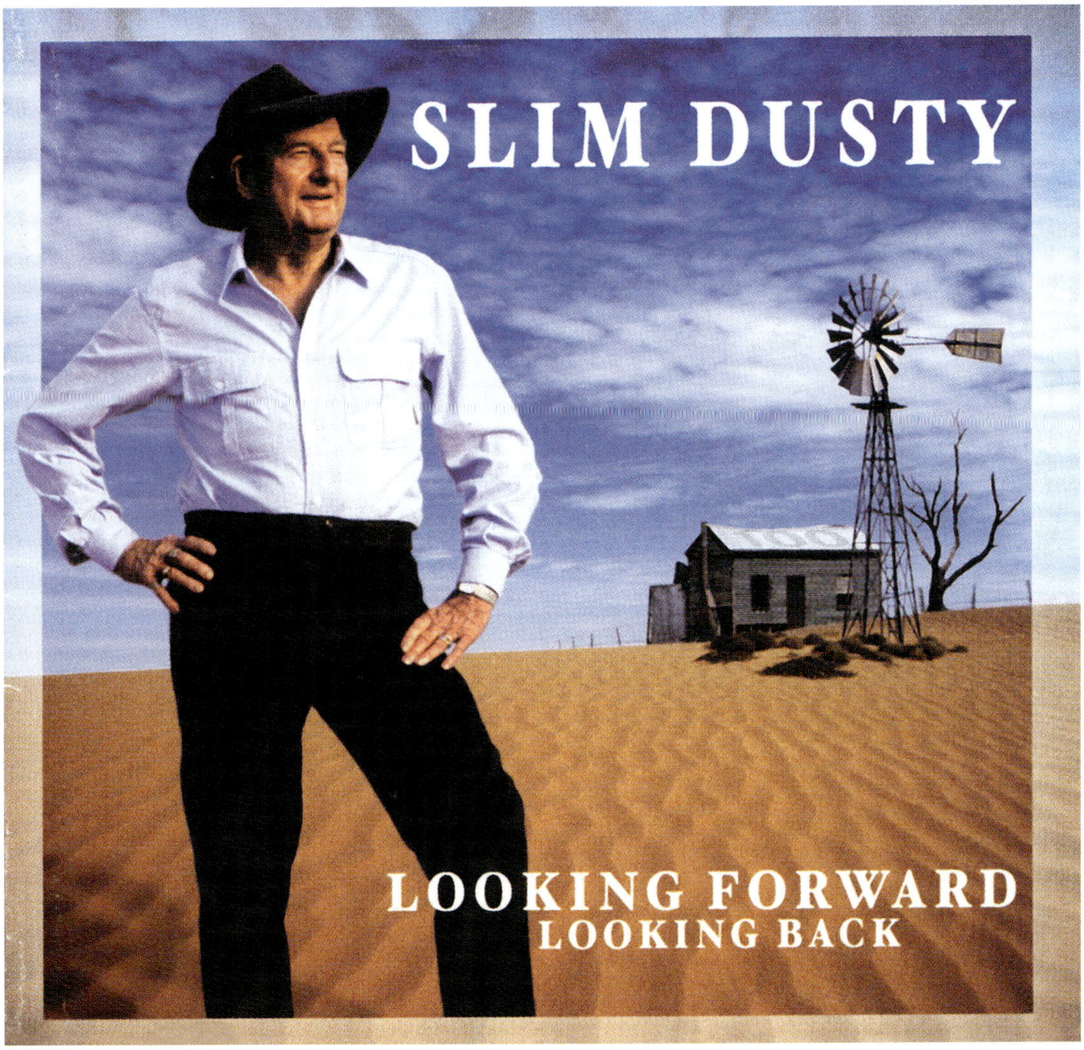

SLIM DUSTY
LOOKING FORWARD
LOOKING BACK

## WEST OF WINTON

'This shot was taken in the main street of Winton outside the Waltzing Matilda Centre. That's Banjo Paterson in the background. The title track was written by Ray Rose who was the butcher in Winton at one time.'

WEST OF WINTON
SLIM DUSTY

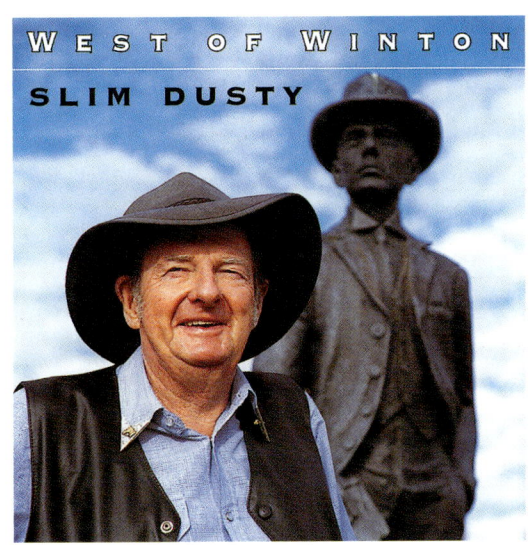

# You Can't Keep a Good Man Down

Picture the scene: Slim and his Travelling Country Band are on stage at the Empire Theatre in Toowoomba and they are cooking. Slim is pumping, obviously loving what he is doing. He has the crowd of fourteen hundred fans hanging off his every word. Song after song, every one of them a well-known Slim Dusty hit.

**LEFT**  At Rangelands, just outside Winton, western Queensland

His fans demand to hear so many songs that Slim Dusty, over the years, has gotten into the habit of singing medleys of his hits so he can fit them all into a concert performance.

Looking at Slim on stage it is hard to imagine that he was born in '27, and even harder to imagine that he's had life-threatening heart surgery.

Earlier in 1999, just before the Tamworth Festival in January, Slim was given the news that he had a serious problem with his heart. Slim, seventy-one at the time, handled the situation like any other problem that has cropped up over his fifty-year career.

'If I need surgery, let's do it,' Slim said. 'That's the way I've always been. If something needs doing, let's do it!'

**RIGHT** The family backstage at the Tamworth Town Hall, 2002 – Slim and Joy with son David and daugher Anne and granddaughters Hannah, thirteen, and Kate, twenty

## *That's the way I've always been. If something needs doing, let's do it!*

Slim's son David is a doctor and having him on hand to arrange things was one of the reasons Slim faced this crisis so calmly. 'I didn't have much time to think about it and that was the way I wanted it. I said to my family, get me in the ambulance and get to the hospital, and the following day they wheeled me in for the operation.'

Within four days of entering the Royal North Shore Private Hospital in Sydney Slim's heart operation was done and within six days he was back on his feet.

'I must mention that the nurses, sisters, and doctors at the Royal North Shore Private Hospital did a great job. I knew I was in for a serious operation, I knew I had to rest and watch myself after the operation,' Slim said philosophically. 'They were so organised and did everything so well. They made me feel right at home.'

Slim is very thankful for the treatment he received. 'The medical people, hospital, nurses and doctors, they deserve as much credit and help, financially and every other way, that our country can give them. A lot of politicians don't realise how important the health of nation is. It is just as important as the defence of our nation.'

Slim says that he never considered giving up his busy life of recording and performing his beloved bush ballads. 'I was too busy trying to stack all the cards and get well wishes that came from the Tamworth Festival to my hospital room, all the flowers and stuff that came in. I got a great kick out of seeing some of the write-ups in the papers. One bloke with a guitar over his back was wearing a t-shirt that said, "Get Well Slim". My old mate Paul Donkin came in every second day; I was jumping up, he was trying to make me sit down. After about the first night when my dinner came in they asked if I would like a stubby or a glass of wine. I thought this is a bloody good hospital.'

It was only a matter of a couple of months to recuperate and Slim was back doing what he loved, taking his show on the road and performing for his fans.

'My first concert back was at Dubbo; it was a good night,' Slim remembers. 'I had a

ABOVE Kate and
Hannah join Joy and
Slim on stage

bit of a queer feeling when we went back on the road. We did a reasonable length tour down into South Australia and then to places we had missed in Victoria and Tasmania. We had to do these concerts in the really cold winter to keep faith with my fans. We went down through Ballarat and Warrnambool. It was freezing but it was one of the best tours that I can remember. The crowds came, we had a good time.'

Arthur Laing is Slim Dusty's promoter and long-time friend. 'On the last two tours, the number of tickets we pre-sold was out of the ordinary', Arthur said. 'Concerts were sold out two weeks in advance and this just hasn't happened before.'

Asked to sum up Slim's appeal, Arthur answered, 'He's an old bastard and people love that. I think there is something special about him. His voice is unique; the way he has always presented himself is unique. He sings every single song from his heart. He's always managed to get great songs and present them in the best possible way.'

Although Slim has been known to have the odd drink now and then, his first tour back after his illness was the first time in years that there were regular after-concert parties. 'We got invited back to lots of pubs for private parties after our shows,' Slim said. 'The boys from the band brought their instruments and we all had a jam. It was one

**LEFT** One of the few times Slim hasn't played guitar on stage was when Lee Kernaghan helped him out at the Tamworth Awards in 1993. Slim was recovering from surgery to his shoulder

of the best tours we had in years. It was a good comeback, a very happy one. Everyone was pleased to see me.'

After a lifetime on the road Slim is still amazed at the way people treat him. 'I am so deeply appreciative of the support from everyone. Sometimes when I finish a show I am in a hurry to get away but parents will jump up on the stage after you and they have got children three and four years old. The little bloke's dressed up and he is running after you to get an autograph signed. It just makes you feel you can't give up when people feel like that about you.'

Arthur Laing explains why he thinks Slim is performing better than he ever has. 'When

you get a shock like Slim did with his heart problem you tend to have a different perspective on life. Slim has always enjoyed playing and now he enjoys it even more. I think he realises what he may have missed if he hadn't had that operation.'

Two years on and Slim has had another health scare. Tests carried out in November 2001 uncovered a tumour on his left kidney and he had surgery to remove the kidney. Slim quickly recuperated after the surgery and his doctor said, 'Slim's prognosis is excellent and he should be back to full health inside a couple of weeks'.

Two months later, the Tamworth Town Hall was the scene for Slim's triumphant

**RIGHT** Anne
Kirkpatrick and her
daughter Kate

**BELOW** Slim and the
Travelling Country
Band

**FOLLOWING PAGES** Slim's iconic hat is an Akubra Sundowner that Akubra no longer manufacture for sale. However, they make a dozen at a time when slim needs them! These shots show Slim breaking in a brand new Sundowner

return from the 'dead'. People had heard about Slim's surgery to remove the kidney, with the papers claiming he was sick and would never tour again. But Slim's wife Joy McKean told the crowd, 'Slim is not dead, this is not his last show and he will continue to tour'. The fans went wild. 'Rumours of Slim's demise have been greatly exaggerated,' Joy continued. 'I'd like you to welcome him on stage ... Slim Dusty!'

Slim strode confidently onto the stage and there was a roar of relief from the thousand-strong crowd. The fans saw him at his best and they were thrilled! The show was a corker, with Slim and The Travelling Country Band dishing up dozens of country classics. The night was extra special because the Dusty family had travelled to Tamworth to support Slim.

Performing on the night were the yodelling McKean Sisters – Joy and her sister Heather, daughter Anne Kirkpatrick, son David, who as well as being a full-time doctor is also a very talented singer and guitar player, Anne's daughter Kate, twenty, and David's daughter Hannah, thirteen.

Joy had the final word after Slim's performance, telling everyone: 'The only time you will get Slim off stage is if you drag him off by his boots!'

*The fans went wild. 'Rumours of Slim's demise have been greatly exaggerated,' Joy continued.*

# Slim's Road Songs

Most Slim Dusty songs feature a strong sense of 'place' and for years in my travels I keep myself amused by matching up the passing landscape with Slim Dusty songs. I fondly recall driving into Camooweal early one cool winter's morning listening to 'Camooweal', the song written by Mack Cormack. It gave me goose bumps. Every time I see a gum tree by the roadway, Slim's song of the same name instantly comes to mind. I can't sit by a fire of gidgee coals without humming the song that Coster wrote for Slim. Slim has documented his life through his songs and many of these songs are about Slim's life on the road. Here is a selection of Slim's 'road songs' matched up with my photos.

# Another Day Another Town

## SLIM DUSTY

There was old G.P. an' Joy and me sittin' round the motel door

Talkin' about the day ahead and the show the night before

You know it sums it up to me because tomorrow's gone and dead

No lookin' back there's too many good times waiting up ahead

May there always be an endless road that I can ramble down

May there always be another day that leads to another town

It's satisfaction still for me to be just movin' round

When I can say it's another day … another town

This is old G.P. and you know me I just went sliding out

To some pubs and shows back in the town when Slim went heading south

I've said a lot of goodbyes in this crazy life of mine

But when I meet a mate out on the road we make up for lost time

Now the stay at homes say rolling stones will never gather moss

To all of that I answer back just say who wants moss

So if I ever reach that golden stage up in the promised land

Oh I'll quickly book myself a string the good old western town

# On the Move Again

## JOY McKEAN

With my travellin' country band
I cover this old land
And nothin' suits so well
As when I'm movin'
Rehearsal is all done
The show is set to run
So load the truck
Pack your gear and get movin'
Leave studios behind
There's nothin' on my mind
But knowin' that at last
I can get movin'
I've done all that I should
And I've done the best I could
Now it's all gotta happen
'Cause I'm movin'
I'm on the move again
The world is good again
And as I pull out I hear the
    phone ring
In the empty hall

But I've done everything
So I just let it ring
And for better or for worse
I'm on the move again
No way could I believe
In a better way to live
If I didn't take my songs
And get them movin'
Songs meant to be sung
And shared with everyone
I wonder if that's why
I keep on movin'
So close the office desk
Pack the new songs with the rest
And neither love nor money
Stops my movin'
Oh I've given it a try
Now someone tell me why
I should live beside a phone
And never move again
No way

# Finally Made it Home

## ANDY OTES AND SLIM DUSTY

I finally made it home and I'll be stayin'
Nothin's gonna make me change my mind
I just saw the first of many landmarks
The opening of the old abandoned mine
I can't wait to see the old familiar faces
As we come in the main street of our town
The truckie here beside me says I'll see you
I thank him for the lift and jump on down
I head straight for the pub and nearly miss it
They've done it up and there's carpet on the floor
Lots of plastic tables and strange faces
The old upright piano's gone for sure
I take a look around for someone I might know
Ask the barmaid about some friends of mine
She looks at me peculiar, all she does is shrug
I doubt if she would give a man the time
At least the beer was good so I have another
With a special counter lunch and then some smokes
I helped the owner pay for his new carpet
And his fancy prices sure would send you broke
I walk around my town but it's so different
The produce store's a supermarket now
Ah but mostly I see people in a hurry
And where they used to smile they only frown
I finally made it home but I can't stay here
It's changed so much I had to change my mind
Oh the town is full of faces but they're empty
As empty as the old abandoned mine

# Highway Blues

## SLIM DUSTY

I'm gonna put my foot down on the gas
  and just pretend I could not care less
And that's the way I'm a gonna lose
  these lonely highway blues
Well I left behind a girl or two
  never found one to be true
Whoever makes me want to lose
  these lonely highway blues
Guess that I will never change
  never lose the thrill
Wonderin' what's around the bend
  or over the very next hill
I'm gonna put my foot down on the gas
  and just pretend I could not care less
And that's the way I'm gonna lose
  these lonely highway blues
I've been a restless rambler since knee high
  open road and open sky
I guess it's too darn late to lose
  these lonely highway blues

Well I left behind a girl or two
  never found one to be true
Whoever makes me want to lose
  these lonely highway blues
The sun comes up and the sun goes
  down to me it's all the same
Today I'm movin' up the hill
  tomorrow I'm out on the plain
I'm gonna put my foot down on the gas
  and just pretend I could not care less
And that's the way I'm a gonna lose
  these lonely highway blues
The sun comes up and the sun goes down
  to me it's all the same
Today I'm movin' up the hill
  tomorrow I'm out on the plain
I'm gonna put my foot down on the gas
  and just pretend I could not care less
And that's the way I'm a gonna lose
  these lonely highway blues

# What Am I Doing in this Town?

**JOY McKEAN**

One main street, one hotel if you're lucky
The general store just closed the door
    and you find you got no bread
The road you travelled had more corrugations
    than a tin roof
It's not your day in any way
    and how you wished you'd stayed in bed
You walk up to the pub verandah slowly
But don't move too fast when you go past
    that ol' blue heeler hound
Keep facin' him until you think
    you can beat him to the doorway
And ask yourself just what the hell
    you're doing in this town
What am I doing in this town
I just landed here and maybe
    they don't want me round
Hey tell me what am I doing in this town
Find the man who has the key to the town hall
You'd think that it was made of gold
    the way he carries on
Says don't forget to leave it clean
    same way as you find it
Well it won't be hard
I'll just forget to sweep it when I'm gone
Oh you camp beside the stage door
    where there's no shade
Park the car get your guitar
    put seats out in a row

The empty stage is dusty
    and the curtain's just not working
You read the posters on the wall
    of an old time travelling show
What am I doing in this town
They don't want me here
    and I don't want to stay around
Hey tell me what am I doing in this town
Sun goes down and the lights go on in the
    windows
Turn on every light
    we've got and play the music loud
Once again the magic comes
    across the yellow footlights
And every song you sing
    you give your soul out to the crowd
Oh some may come to laugh and some to listen
Or maybe bring a story
    they know you'd like to hear.
You feel at home on every stage
    at every town you come to
And you know the answer
    when you ask the same thing every year
What am I doing in this town
I feel welcome here
I feel I've got good friends around
I tell ya
That's what I'm doing in this town
That's what I'm doing in this town

# Traveller's Prayer

## ROD BOUCHER

May the road rise up to meet you
May the wind be always at your back
May the sun shine warm upon your face
And the rain fall soft upon your track
And until, until we meet again
May God hold you safe in the palm of His hands
May the hills come down to greet you
May the rocks give shelter in the storm
May the dust be soft beneath your feet
And the dark give rest before the dawn
And until, until we meet again
May God hold you safe in the palm of His hands
In the palm of His hands
In the palm of His hands
In the palm of His hand
Safely in the palm of His hands
May your life have many memories
May your death be sweet and full of peace
May your hope last an eternity
And your joy carry on and never cease
And until, until we meet again
May God hold you safely in the palm of His hands
And until, until we meet again
May God hold you safely in the palm of His hands
In the palm of His hands
In the palm of His hands
In the palm of His hands
Safely in the palm of His hands

# The Front Row

## JOY McKEAN

Well they're sitting in the front row
   once again
They were there last year when
   hardly no one came
And when we were trying hard
to make the people understand
They were singing right along giving
   us a hand
From the front row
Everybody else was wearin' easy kind
   of clothes
She wore silk and him a velvet coat
Oh it made us feel
like we were special in a special show
Didn't have to say a word just let
   us know
From the front row
And the faces in the front row
come from every walk of life
Each one has a story to tell
They don't know that from the stage

I see them all so clear
And sometimes can read their
   thoughts as well
Well their faces are transparent
when they listen to your song
Their minds are years away
for now they're free
From the ordinary body in the
   ordinary chair
They're up with you in the floodlights
They're no longer sitting there
In the front row
The quiet little man who often
came through mud and rain
If he was late, the old car took the
   blame
But he nearly always made it
he never would be beat
Until this year got beyond him
and I see an empty seat
in the front row

# Walk a Country Mile

## JOY McKEAN

Well I've walked a mile or two in my lifetime

And I've travelled down some muddy tracks and dry

'Cause if I wanted to get where I was going

I knew I'd just have to walk that country mile

Now a country mile would be the longest distance

A man could ever travel when he's down

And you curse the never ending road before you

When you think you'll never make it into town

But you meet a friend or two along the highway

And you learn a lot you never knew before

And if the journey takes a lifetime

When you thought a year or two

Well you just don't give up easy any more

Walkin' that long mile has shown me changes

Changes in the people and the land

But I bet the road to Marble Bar's no better

Than when I drove with trucks and caravans

And the country bloke is still the same old battler

No matter what the place he's workin' in

And although I've covered many miles

I still can't wait to see

What the next long country mile will bring

Yes I knew I'd have to walk that country mile

# The Biggest Disappointment

**JOY McKEAN**

They had my future wrapped up in a parcel

And no one even thought of asking me

The day I turned fifteen I caught the mail train

To find what else might be in life for me

I rode on trucks and trains and lived on nothin'

Served me right for wanting to be free

Ah well that's the way society looked at it

But it didn't seem to be that way to me

And the biggest disappointment in the family was me

The only twisted branch upon our good old family tree

I just couldn't be the person they expected me to be

And the biggest disappointment in the world was me

A lot more dinner times than there were dinners

I learned a lot that hurt me at the time

Then this quiet country boy went home a different man

With a memory of distance on my mind

But I always spoke too loud and laughed too often

Maybe drank too many glasses down

And perhaps my clothes were older than I realised

A relief to all concerned when I left town

And the biggest disappointment in the family was me

The only twisted branch upon our good old family tree

I just couldn't be the person they expected me to be

And the biggest disappointment in the world was me

# Memory Motel

## ALISTAIR JONES

Check into the motel hang your coat behind the door

Like so many travellers who've passed this way before

Well it may have been in '55 or '63 or 4

The first time that we showed in this old town

Seemed to make each place our home as soon as we arrived

But somewhere all good characters and showmen still survive

Where we meet up after every show and stories come alive

And good company will gather round

And we'll be leaving in the morning there's so many folks to see

We'll be driving maybe flying who can tell

Leave the lights on tonight cause we'll be playing here all right

And we're staying at the Memory Motel

They can build it on the highway or in the heart of town

Somehow every motel seems the same

You can put it on a hill, call it what you will

But the memory motel is now its name

I wonder what the neighbours think in the rooms next door

Of our noises wild and haunting as our banjo player snores

Oh the mad and gleeful laughter over stories from the floor

I sometimes think old Ned's with us again

Our friends from every district call with stubbies, wine and more

And you know you're back out on the track where good times went before

Kick off your shoes but leave your blues and troubles by the door

Yes lighten up mate, you're with friends

And the spirit of a travelling band that's swept across the land

And linger at the Memory Motel

Yes we're staying at the Memory Motel

# Gum Trees by the Roadway

## SLIM DUSTY

Tonight here by the roadside after driving hard all day

Dreaming of the old folks and the homestead o'er the way

In dreams I see the old place I'll be there within a week

Where there's gum trees by the roadway and willows by the creek

I see the homestead cattle as around the place they roam

The old man with the horses on the fields of golden loam

And mother in the doorway just to make this scene complete

With gum trees by the roadway and willows by the creek

I'd like to tell my story in a simple kind of way

It happened many hundreds in the war torn world today

I heard the call for duty so I donned a khaki suit

And I marched way from the gum trees and willows by the creek

Now when the war was over and we'd marched the victory mile

The ties with home were broken and from there I stayed a while

I palled up with some fellows just to live on easy street

And forgot about the gum trees and the willows by the creek

Oh but when you land in trouble and you're placed behind those bars

That's when you start thinking of the country moon and stars

When at last they free you and you step out on the street

Oh nothing then could hold you from the homestead by the creek

Well that's why tonight I'm standing by this cheery roadside fire

Taking in the country underneath the summer stars

From now on you will find me where the air is fresh and sweet

Where forever there'll be gum trees and willows by the creek

And willows by the creek

# The Road is Still My Home

## SLIM DUSTY

Oh I miss the trees, the grass and the open skies

Oh you never miss the water, until the well runs dry

In the heart of town that has no heart I feel so all alone

I guess the open road is still my home, sweet home

I guess the open road is still my home

In town in everything you seem to do

There's an endless wait or an endless stand bunched up in a queue

Oh you all seem busy buzzing round like bees in a honeycomb

But it's not for me you can have your honeycomb, sweet comb.

I'll take the open country for my home

So many say why don't you settle down

Oh you must get tired and weary, always moving round

But there's no place in particular where I will stay too long

North or south, east or west is home, sweet home

Australia anywhere is home sweet home

Farewell old friend I'll not be gone too long

Oh you've been my guiding hand, a father to me all along

For many years you've seen me come and go now on the roam

And you know the reason why I have to roam, and roam

Because the open country is my home

When the highway sweeps beneath my restless wheels

There's a surge of happiness that only wanderers can feel

Oh I'm searching for a distant star that ever calls me on

So I guess always the road will be my home, sweet home

I guess always the road will be my home

# I've Been There and Back Again

**JOY McKEAN**

I've been there and back again
while you've been thinking about it
I've had all there was to have
and I've had to do without it
I've had sunshine I've had rain
I've known pleasure, I've known pain
I've been there and back again
Life's not easy on the road
sometimes carry a heavy load
And no one wants to know you
Can't help thinking now and then
better go back home again
But brother mine don't ever let it
 throw you
Take a look at where you're at
home is where you hang your hat
And you're the only one who tells
 you what to do

Rode on trains and trucks before
had to walk till my feet were sore
Gave me time to really look about
Sang my songs just anywhere
stayed if there was room to spare
And overstayed my welcome
 sometimes I've no doubt
Had it easy done it hard
seen a lot of life's back yard
Made mistakes I know
but that's all in the game
I have to smile as I look back
I hear 'em say oh it's tough on
 the track
Maybe so but I know I'd do it
 all again

Yeah I've been there

# I Need to Find a Place

## SLIM DUSTY

I need to find a place
Where I can rest my mind
From this world of just can't wait
Chasing artificial times
I need to find a homestead
Where you can leave an open gate
And the world won't fall and crumble
If you should roll up late
I need to see some river gums
That man has left alone
In some quiet peaceful valley
Where the trees shall shade my home
And I'll be back with Mother Nature
So often it's been told
'I'm the Mother Bush that loves you
Come to me when you are old'
On the big old front verandah
I'll just sing alone and strum
And throw away this timepiece

And take my bearings from the sun
And then later in the evening
When the world is half awake
I'll see the glory of the bushland
When the big moon comes up late
I need to see some river gums
That man has left alone
In some quiet peaceful valley
Where the trees will shade my home
Yes I need to find a place
From the madness and the rush
And I'll be back with Mother Nature
In the bosom of the bush
Oh I need to find a place
Where I can rest my mind
From this world of just can't wait
Chasing artificial kinds
I need to find a place

# Travellin' Guitar

## SLIM DUSTY

All my life I've been a traveller

Movin' near and far

And my friend each day along the way

Has been my travelling' guitar

From a free life in the country

To the city's rush and jar

And when things were bad

I always had my faithful travellin' guitar

'Long the road of song I've travelled

It's sometimes a road of chance

Had my ups and downs, laughs and frowns

And share of broken romance

Sydney Sue was my first romance

She just loved my two-toned guitar

But her Dad, the lout, kicked us out

Me and my travellin' guitar

All my life has been a gamble

Hitched to a distant star

But my greatest friend around each bend

Has been my travellin' guitar

When it's time to play up yonder

And I'm billed as a star

Will I find a place with the chosen race

For me and my travellin' guitar

# The Long Road

## SLIM DUSTY

It's been a long road of song

We have travelled

Some miles blessed with joy

Some marked with tears

But in harmony we've made it together

And that's how we'll face future years

Let's be thankful for the joys we have tasted

For true friends and a family that's worthwhile

Such a long road of song

We have travelled

And we wouldn't change one single mile

We can laugh

At our early days of travel

At all the many things

That we did wrong

Our worldly possessions were so humble

But our faith in each other moved us on

And we still have a steep grade to follow

Country music seems to make it all worthwhile

And the road of song will always

Be a calling

And we'll always live and love

Each country mile

# Born to be a Rolling Stone

## SLIM DUSTY

As the years roll along I tramp along beside them

Never have no cares, so never need to hide them

From the sunny north down to the south I roam

For I guess that I was born a rolling stone

Sometimes I settle down and the road forgets me

So I down tools and I just leave work alone

For I guess that I was born a rolling stone

My mates are far and many

As I tramp throughout the year

Some are rich and some are poor

But over a glass of beer

They're all decent blokes

Who share a joke

With no distinction shown

And they're the mates

Of this old rolling stone

How my life has changed, to me it seems like magic

From what I used to be, some say it's tragic

Oh but that's a story better left alone

For I guess that I was born a rolling stone

So when I'm on the track and camped beside the highway

Just a lazin' back and gazin' at God's skyway

Will my footsteps ever reach that golden throne

Will they ever welcome in this rolling stone

# Just Going Home

## SLIM DUSTY

This story I must tell you
Is old and very true
And when it comes around your door
It always seems so new
I've had my share of hardships
And success while on the roam
Now the year has ended once again
And I'm just going home
Ten long months on the road of song
I'm saddle weary now
Gonna brush the cobwebs from
  my eyes
And the wrinkles from my brow
Can't stay to talk, must be on my way
And leave your town alone
Oh it's very important now, you know
'Cause I'm just going home

I've never seen the skies so blue
The sun is warm and bright
I'm friends with everyone I see
My world is spinnin' right
I'm travelling down to Homewood
That friendly peaceful zone
This world can go on rushing by
I'm just going home
Let me laze around the barbecue
At the closing of the day
And I see the big moon rising high
Across old Bancroft Bay
And hear the bellbirds calling
Their friendly tinkling tone
It's my paradise and I know I'm right
And I'm just going home

# Travellin' Still ... Always Will

## ANNE KIRKPATRICK

Well he left the farm and the
    family home
To follow his boyhood dream
She loved her plays and poetry
Who'd have thought they'd make
    a team

Her sister said he's wild at heart
With his hat turned down in front
But 'twas a passionate turn of
    the heart
That led them down that country mile

Together their star would shine
    so bright
Travellin' through the darkest night
Together they'd climb the highest high
Travellin' still always will

He had his best mates Ned and Joe
And together they'd roam the towns
High times they were young

And wild doing the music rounds
'Twas there he met the sisters
with one he fell in  love
And she gave up the Melody Trail
To walk another one

Together yet so different
But the years have told their tale
How they pioneered a travellin' way
    of life
Sometimes it makes me wonder has
    it come
At such a price
... I think it might

Together their star would shine
    so bright
Travellin' through the darkest night
Together they'd climb the highest high
Travellin' still always will

# Slim's Career Highlights

Slim Dusty continues to amaze. Hot on the heels of his double-platinum-selling 100th album, *Looking Forward, Looking Back*, and his spine-tingling performance of 'Waltzing Matilda' at the closing ceremony of the 2000 Olympics, Slim's star shines brighter than ever.

**LEFT** Slim with his trademarks: the distinctive Akubra and his Maton guitar

| | |
|---|---|
| **1927** | Born Kempsey, 13 June. Named David Gordon Kirkpatrick. Raised nearby at Nulla Nulla Creek dairy farm. |
| **1937** | Aged ten writes first song, 'The Way the Cowboy Dies'. |
| **1938** | Calls himself Slim Dusty. |
| **1942** | Performs on Radio 2KM Kempsey. Makes his first recording at own expense – 'Song for the Aussies' and 'My Final Song'. |
| **1945** | Still living at Nulla Nulla Creek, writes his first country music classic 'When the Rain Tumbles Down in July'. |
| **1946** | Signs first recording contract with the Columbia Gramophone Co. for the Regal Zonophone label. Slim records six titles including 'When the Rain Tumbles Down in July'. |
| **1948-54** | Part-time show business career intermittent radio, hall shows and tent appearances. |
| **1951** | Marries country singer–songwriter Joy McKean. |
| **1952** | Daughter Anne Kirkpatrick born. |
| **1954** | Commences full-time show business career. Launches first travelling Slim Dusty Show. |
| **1956** | Establishes partnership with showman Frankie Foster, which established the Slim Dusty Show as a large tent show on the show-ground circuit. |
| **1957** | Records 'A Pub With No Beer' – at that time the biggest selling record ever by an Australian. |
| **1958** | Son David Kirkpatrick born. Received Australia's first Gold record for 'A Pub With No Beer'. |
| **1960** | Release of first album *Slim Dusty Sings*. |
| **1963** | Ends show-ground partnership with Frankie Foster. |
| **1964** | Establishes annual round Australia Slim Dusty tour – a fifty-thousand kilometre, ten-month journey. |
| **1969** | First tour outside Australia, in New Zealand with NZ's Hamilton County Bluegrass Band. Also tours Papua New Guinea and Solomon Islands. |
| **1970** | Awarded an MBE for services to music. |
| **1973** | Tamworth's first Australasian Country Music Awards. Awarded Best LP for *Me and My Guitar*. Best EP or single for 'Lights on the Hill'. |
| **1978** | First Sydney Opera House performance. |
| **1979** | Daughter Anne awarded Best Female Vocalist at Tamworth while wife Joy was awarded Best Composition for 'Beat Of The Government Stroke'. Slim elevated to the Roll of Renown. |
| **1979** | Publishes bestselling autobiography *Walk a Country Mile*. Identically titled album has achieved Platinum status in sales. |
| **1980** | Records super-hit 'Duncan', achieving Gold status. |

**LEFT**  In 1999, Slim was featured on the popular television show, 'This is Your Life'

1981   *The Golden Anniversary Album*, Slim's fifty-first release, reaches Multi-Platinum status in Australia.

1984   Release of feature film *The Slim Dusty Movie*.

1986   In November, celebrated forty years of commercial recording with the one company, EMI Music Australia. Slim's latest album, *Beer Drinking Songs of Australia*, went Gold in the first three weeks of release.

1987   At Tamworth Country Music Awards of Australia, trucking album *Neon City* won Album of the Year.
       Slim Dusty is inducted into the ARIA Hall of Fame on 29 February.

1989   Heritage Award for 'We've Done Us Proud'. Album *G'day, G'Day* goes Gold. Records first duet album with daughter Anne Kirkpatrick.

1990   Appears in Papua New Guinea as Australia's representative at the Southern Highlands Province's Independence Celebrations. Takes his show around Australia.

1991   *Two Singers One Song* duet album awarded Best Selling Album at Tamworth Music Festival and *Coming Home* takes out Best Album of the Year Award. 19 November marks the forty-fifth anniversary of his first commercial recording, *When the Rain Tumbles Down in July*.

1992   Involved in the formation of the Country Music Association of Australia. Recorded top-selling video *Live into the Nineties*.

1993   Fiftieth anniversary of continuous recording in Australia. As guest of Aboriginal band Yothu Yindi, Slim and his band tour all the Northern Territory and Bathurst Island.

**RIGHT** These are just
some of the many
Gold records Slim
and Joy have
received. Ultimately
they will be housed
at the proposed
museum at Kempsey

| | |
|---|---|
| **1994** | Celebrates forty years of touring. |
| | Wins Golden Guitar with Lee Kernaghan for Vocal Group or Duo with 'Leave Him in the Longyard'. |
| | Tours New Zealand. |
| | Slim presented with a Double Platinum Award for sales in excess of 20 000 video cassettes for *Slim Dusty – Live into the Nineties* and with a Platinum Award for sales in excess of 10 000 video cassettes for *Slim Dusty – Across Australia*. |
| **1995** | On 20 January the Slim Dusty Exhibition opened for a twelve-month period at the Australian Country Music Foundation Museum in Tamworth. |
| **1996** | Slim is presented with the Special Achievement Award by ARIA. |
| **1997** | Slim completes his ninety-first album and an accompanying long-form video recording, both aptly named *91 Over 50*. |
| **1998** | Celebrates his jubilee of commercial recording with EMI at the Regent Hotel in Sydney. |
| | Publishes new autobiography, *Another Day, Another Town*. |
| | Tours England and Ireland for the first time to sellout crowds. |
| | EMI Music designs and builds a full professional studio facility in Slim and Joy's backyard. |
| | In October, Slim releases his ninety-ninth album appropriately titled *'99*. |
| | Slim named Father of the Year and Senior Australian of the Year. |

Slim appears live as a special invited guest on the Grand Ole Opry in Nashville, Tennessee.

Releases *Makin' a Mile*.

Awarded the AO in the Order of Australia for services to Australian country music and the entertainment industry both as a composer and performer.

1999    Slim and Joy receive Gold Guitars for Bush Ballad of the Year at the CMAA Awards in Tamworth.

*Not So Dusty – A Tribute to Slim Dusty* released, featured acts include Midnight Oil, Paul Kelly, Don Walker, Mental As Anything and The Screaming Jets. Debuts Top 30 in the ARIA pop charts.

Slim headlines the first concert in the new Tamworth Regional Entertainment Centre in front of 5000 people.

2000    Slim records his 100th album – *Looking Forward, Looking Back* – sales quickly reach Double Platinum.

2001    Features on *Living Legend* stamp series for Australia Post.

Golden Guitars for Bush Ballad of the Year with Paddy William, Top Selling Album of the Year for *Looking Forward, Looking Back* and Video Clip of the Year for *Looking Forward, Looking Back*. Release of *West of Winton* and *The Men from Nulla Nulla*, albums number 101 and 102.

2002    Wins Golden Guitar for Bush Ballad of the Year with *West of Winton*.

Releases *Travellin' Still … Always Will*, his 103rd album.

**LEFT** Slim proudly showing the Living Legend stamp series. The other stamp design is one suggested by a country music magazine in the early '90s

# The Official 100 (+3) Slim Dusty Albums

Prolific, incredible, unbelievable – there isn't a word in the English language that does justice to Slim's record of 103 albums and still climbing. Right from day one, back in the '40s, Slim has felt compelled to record. Every year, sometimes several times a year, he makes the now familiar journey back to the recording studio. Now that he has a studio in his backyard, there's every chance he will become even more prolific! The amazing thing is he just keeps getting better and better.

1. SLIM DUSTY SINGS
2. SONGS FOR ROLLING STONES
3. ALONG THE ROAD OF SONG
4. AUSSIE SING SONG
5. SONGS IN THE SADDLE
6. ANOTHER AUSSIE SING SONG
7. SONGS OF AUSTRALIA
8. PEOPLE AND PLACES
9. AUSTRALIAN BUSH BALLADS
10. THE NATURE OF THE MAN

11. AN EVENING WITH SLIM AND JOY
12. ESSENTIALLY AUSTRALIAN
13. THE BEST OF SLIM DUSTY
14. SONGS MY FATHER SANG TO ME
15. SONGS FROM THE CATTLE CAMPS
16. SING ALONG WITH DAD
17. CATTLE CAMP CROONER
18. SLIM DUSTY ENCORES
19. SING A HAPPY SONG
20. SONGS FROM THE LAND I LOVE

21. GLORY BOUND TRAIN
22. LIVE AT WAGGA WAGGA
23. ME AND MY GUITAR
24. FOOLIN' AROUND
25. THE BEST OF SLIM DUSTY / COUNTRY LIVING (WRC)
26. LIVE AT TAMWORTH
27. DUSTY TRACKS
28. TALL STORIES AND SAD SONGS
29. SLIM DUSTY – AUSTRALIANA
30. DINKI DI AUSSIES

31. THE BEST OF SLIM DUSTY (VOL 2)
32. LIGHTS ON THE HILL
33. WAY OUT THERE
34. THINGS I SEE AROUND ME
35. GIVE ME THE ROAD
36. SLIM DUSTY – THIS IS YOUR LIFE

37. SONGS FROM DOWN UNDER

38. JUST SLIM – WITH OLD FRIENDS

39. ON THE MOVE

40. TRAVELLIN' COUNTRY MAN

41. TO WHOM IT MAY CONCERN

42. SLIM DUSTY SINGS HIS FAVOURITE SONGS (2 LP SET/WRC)

43. THE ENTERTAINER (LIVE AT THE SYDNEY OPERA HOUSE)

44. SPIRIT OF AUSTRALIA

45. SLIM DUSTY RARITIES

46. RODEO RIDERS

47. WALK A COUNTRY MILE

48. A GUITAR AND A HAT (3 LP SET/WRC)

49. THE MAN WHO STEADIES THE LEAD

50. SLIM DUSTY FAMILY ALBUM

51. NO 50 – GOLDEN ANNIVERSARY ALBUM

52. WHERE COUNTRY IS

53. VINTAGE ALBUM (VOL 1)

54. WHO'S RIDING OLD HARLEQUIN NOW?

55. VINTAGE ALBUM (VOL 2)

56. ON THE WALLABY

57. I HAVEN'T CHANGED A BIT

58. TRUCKS ON THE TRACK

59. SLIM DUSTY MOVIE (SOUNDTRACK)

60. THE BEST OF SLIM DUSTY (6 LP SET/READER'S DIGEST)

61. I'LL TAKE MINE COUNTRY STYLE

62. SINGER FROM DOWN UNDER

63. TO A MATE (MACK CORMACK)

64. AUSTRALIA IS HIS NAME (3 LP SET)

65. LIVE ACROSS AUSTRALIA

66. STORIES I WANTED TO TELL

67. VINTAGE ALBUM (VOL 3)

68. SLIM DUSTY'S BEER DRINKING SONGS OF AUSTRALIA

69.  NEON CITY
70.  COUNTRY LIVING

71.  CATTLEMEN FROM THE HIGH PLAINS
72.  THE HERITAGE ALBUM
73.  SLIM DUSTY SINGS STAN COSTER
74.  G'DAY G'DAY
75.  KING OF KALGOORLIE
76.  SLIM DUSTY – HENRY LAWSON AND BANJO PATERSON
77.  VINTAGE ALBUM (VOL 4)
78.  TWO SINGERS ONE SONG
79.  COMING HOME
80.  VINTAGE ALBUM (VOL 5)

81.  A LAND HE CALLS OUR OWN
82.  SLIM DUSTY SINGS JOY MCKEAN
83.  TRAVELLIN' GUITAR
84.  LIVE INTO THE '90S
85.  THAT'S THE SONG WE'RE SINGING
86.  RINGER FROM THE TOP END
87.  ANNIVERSARY ALBUM NO 2 (1943–1993)
88.  NATURAL HIGH
89.  COUNTRY WAY OF LIFE
90.  LIVE AT TOWNSVILLE 1956 (THEATRE ROYAL)

91.  COUNTRY CLASSICS (3 CD SET/READER'S DIGEST)
92.  91 OVER 50
93.  A TIME TO REMEMBER
94.  MAKIN' A MILE
95.  TALK ABOUT THE GOOD TIMES
96.  LAND OF LOTS OF TIME – SONGS OF AUSTRALIA (2 CD SET)
97.  DOWN THE DUSTY ROAD – OLD TIME DROVER'S LAMENT (2 CD SET)
98.  THE VERY BEST OF SLIM DUSTY
99.  '99
100.  LOOKING FORWARD, LOOKING BACK

101.  WEST OF WINTON
102.  THE MEN FROM NULLA NULLA – REUNITED AND REVISITED
103.  TRAVELLIN' STILL ... ALWAYS WILL

# Slim's Golden Guitar Collection

Tamworth is a prosperous city in the north-west of New South Wales, about halfway between Sydney and Brisbane on the New England Highway. In the early '70s a group of businessmen in Tamworth were racking their brains – how to get people to visit their town in January when the temperature often soared over 40 degrees?

**LEFT**  Slim on stage at the Tamworth Golden Guitar Awards, 2001. Fellow award-winners Kelly Crosby and Norma O'Hara Murphy are in the background

ax Ellis and John Minson, from local radio station 2TM, suggested a country music festival. The show went ahead and thirty years later it has grown into one of the biggest music festivals in the world.

The festival went on to develop its own awards, originally known as the Australasian Country Music Awards, but now known as the Golden Guitars. The first of them were presented in the un-air-conditioned town hall in January 1973. That year, Joy McKean won the first ever award for writing the song 'Lights on the Hill', Slim won Best Single for the same song and Slim Newton won Best Selling Record for 'Red Back On The Toilet Seat'. Winning a Golden Guitar is an important milestone in any artist's career. A Golden Guitar can kick start the career of a new artist and can revitalise the career of a well-established one.

Over the years since the awards began, they have been presented in a circus tent, an ambulance factory, the Workman's Club, a high school hall and a rodeo arena. The show itself finally found a permanent home in 1998 at the Tamworth Regional Entertainment Centre. Slim has been a finalist or winner in the awards every year he has been nominated. The list that follows is perfect testament to his talent and the regard in which he is held.

**LEFT** No flash celebrations after the 1997 Golden Guitar Awards – Slim had a cuppa at a Tamworth truck stop

**RIGHT** Slim and
Norma O'Hara
Murphy collected the
Bush Ballad of the
Year Golden Guitar
for Norma's song
'Paddy William'

1973      Album of the Year: *Me and My Guitar.*

Best EP or Single: 'Lights on the Hill'.

(Plus Golden Guitar to Joy McKean for Song of the Year, 'Lights on the Hill',
recorded by Slim).

1974      Album of the Year: *Live at Tamworth.*

1975      Album of the Year: *Slim Dusty – Australiana.*

Male Vocalist of the Year: 'Biggest Disappointment'.

(Plus Golden Guitar to Joy McKean for Song of the Year, 'Biggest
Disappointment' recorded by Slim.)

1976      Top Selling Single: 'Worst in the World'.

Album of the Year: *Lights on the Hill.*

1977      Top Selling Single: 'Things I See Around Me'.

Album of the Year: *Give Me the Road.*

Male Vocalist of the Year: 'Angel Of Goulburn Hill'.

(Plus Golden Guitar to Stan Coster for Song of the Year, 'Three Rivers Hotel',
recorded by Slim.)

1978      Top Selling Single: 'Indian Pacific'.

(Plus Golden Guitar to Joy McKean for Song of the Year, 'Indian Pacific',
recorded by Slim.)

**LEFT** Golden Guitar winners on stage at the Tamworth awards in 1994. From left, Pixie Jenkins, Slim, Gina Jeffreys, Greg Champion, Beccy Cole, Garth Porter and Lee Kernaghan. Slim and Lee shared the Duo of the Year Golden Guitar for 'Leave Him in the Longyard'

1979    Male Vocalist of the Year: *Marty.*
        (Plus Golden Guitar to Tom Oliver and Joy McKean for Song of the Year,
        'Beat of the Government Stroke', recorded by Slim.)
        Elevation to Roll of Renown.
1980    Top Selling Single: 'Walk a Country Mile'.
        Album of the Year: *Walk a Country Mile.*
1981    Top Selling Single: 'The Man who Steadies the Lead'.
        Album of the Year: *The Man who Steadies the Lead.*
1982    Heritage Award: *Where Country is.*
1983    Heritage Award: 'Banjo's Man'.
1984    Album of the Year: *On the Wallaby.*
        Heritage Award: *On the Wallaby.*
1985    Top Selling Single: 'Trucks on the Track'.
        Album of the Year: *Trucks on the Track.*
1987    Heritage Award: 'Mount Bukaroo'.
        (Plus Golden Guitar to Stan Coster for Song of the Year, 'He's a Good Bloke
        When He's Sober', recorded by Slim.)
1988    Album of the Year: *Neon City.*

| | |
|---|---|
| 1989 | Heritage Award: 'We've Done us Proud'. |
| | (Plus Golden Guitar to Graeme Connors for Song of the Year, 'We've Done us Proud', recorded by Slim.) |
| 1991 | Top Selling Single: 'Two Singers One Song' (with Anne Kirkpatrick). |
| | Album of the Year: *Coming Home*. |
| 1992 | Golden Guitar to Bill Chambers for Song of the Year, 'Things are not the Same on the Land', recorded by Slim. |
| 1994 | Vocal Group or Duo of the Year: 'Leave him in the Longyard', with Lee Kernaghan. |
| 1997 | Bush Ballad of the Year: 'Must've Been a Hell of a Party', written by Slim Dusty and Tom Oliver. |
| | Heritage Song of the Year: 'Old Time Country Halls'. |
| 1998 | Bush Ballad of the Year: 'Lady is a Truckie', written by Joy McKean. |
| 2001 | Top Selling Album of the Year: *Looking Forward, Looking Back*. |
| | Video Clip of the Year: *Looking Forward, Looking Back*. |
| | Bush Ballad of the Year: 'Paddy William', written by Norma O'Hara Murphy. |
| 2002 | Bush Ballad of the Year: 'West of Winton', written by Ray Rose. |
| | To date, Slim's record stands at an amazing thirty-five Golden Guitars! |

**RIGHT** 2001 Golden Guitar winners – Slim, Beccy Cole, Adam Brand, Felicity, Sara Storer and Brendon Walmsley. Slim added three Golden Guitars to his collection that year